Blockchain in Inventory Management:

Revolutionizing Transparency, Traceability, and Efficiency

BLOCKCHAIN IN INVENTORY MANAGEMENT: REVOLUTIONIZING TRANSPARENCY, TRACEABILITY, AND EFFICIENCY

CHAPTER 1: INTRODUCTION TO BLOCKCHAIN AND INVENTORY MANAGEMENT

CHAPTER 2: THE EVOLUTION OF BLOCKCHAIN IN SUPPLY CHAINS

- HISTORICAL DEVELOPMENT OF BLOCKCHAIN IN SUPPLY CHAINS
- BLOCKCHAIN'S SHIFT FROM CRYPTOCURRENCY TO INVENTORY APPLICATIONS
- INDUSTRY DRIVERS FOR BLOCKCHAIN ADOPTION IN INVENTORY MANAGEMENT

CHAPTER 3: CORE PRINCIPLES OF BLOCKCHAIN TECHNOLOGY

- DECENTRALIZATION, IMMUTABILITY, AND TRANSPARENCY
- TYPES OF BLOCKCHAINS: PUBLIC, PRIVATE, AND CONSORTIUM
- HOW BLOCKCHAIN'S CORE FEATURES BENEFIT INVENTORY MANAGEMENT

CHAPTER 4: CURRENT CHALLENGES IN INVENTORY MANAGEMENT

- ISSUES IN TRADITIONAL INVENTORY SYSTEMS (E.G., FRAUD, DATA INACCURACY, DELAYS)
- LACK OF VISIBILITY AND ACCOUNTABILITY
- HOW BLOCKCHAIN CAN ADDRESS THESE PAIN POINTS

CHAPTER 5: BLOCKCHAIN ARCHITECTURE AND ITS COMPONENTS

- ➢ **KEY COMPONENTS: DISTRIBUTED LEDGER, BLOCKS, NODES, AND CONSENSUS MECHANISMS**
- ➢ **BLOCKCHAIN DATA STORAGE AND ACCESS MODELS**
- ➢ **SMART CONTRACTS: ENABLING AUTOMATED INVENTORY TRANSACTIONS**

CHAPTER 6: SMART CONTRACTS FOR AUTOMATED INVENTORY MANAGEMENT

- ➢ **OVERVIEW OF SMART CONTRACTS IN BLOCKCHAIN**
- ➢ **BENEFITS OF AUTOMATION IN INVENTORY REORDERING AND STOCK MANAGEMENT**
- ➢ **REAL-WORLD APPLICATIONS OF SMART CONTRACTS IN INVENTORY CONTROL**

CHAPTER 7: DIGITAL TOKENS AND ASSET MANAGEMENT IN INVENTORY

- ➢ **UNDERSTANDING TOKENS AS INVENTORY UNITS**
- ➢ **DIGITAL REPRESENTATION OF INVENTORY ASSETS ON BLOCKCHAIN**
- ➢ **USING TOKENIZATION FOR BETTER ASSET TRACKING AND MANAGEMENT**

CHAPTER 8: INVENTORY TRACKING AND TRACEABILITY WITH BLOCKCHAIN

- ➢ **REAL-TIME TRACKING ACROSS THE SUPPLY CHAIN**
- ➢ **BLOCKCHAIN'S ROLE IN ENSURING TRACEABILITY AND AUTHENTICITY**
- ➢ **BENEFITS OF TRACEABILITY FOR PRODUCT RECALLS AND QUALITY ASSURANCE**

CHAPTER 9: BLOCKCHAIN AND IOT INTEGRATION FOR INVENTORY MANAGEMENT

- ➢ **ROLE OF IOT DEVICES IN COLLECTING INVENTORY DATA**
- ➢ **IOT SENSORS AND BLOCKCHAIN FOR REAL-TIME MONITORING**
- ➢ **CASE EXAMPLES OF BLOCKCHAIN-IOT INTEGRATED INVENTORY SYSTEMS**

CHAPTER 10: ENHANCING DATA SECURITY AND PRIVACY IN INVENTORY

- BLOCKCHAIN'S SECURITY FEATURES: DATA ENCRYPTION, IMMUTABLE LEDGERS
- ENSURING DATA PRIVACY AND CONFIDENTIALITY IN INVENTORY RECORDS
- COMPLIANCE WITH DATA PROTECTION REGULATIONS

CHAPTER 11: FRAUD PREVENTION AND RISK REDUCTION WITH BLOCKCHAIN

- CHALLENGES OF FRAUD IN TRADITIONAL INVENTORY SYSTEMS
- BLOCKCHAIN FOR ENHANCED VERIFICATION AND FRAUD DETECTION
- REDUCING RISKS OF COUNTERFEIT PRODUCTS IN THE SUPPLY CHAIN

CHAPTER 12: BLOCKCHAIN IN QUALITY CONTROL AND COMPLIANCE MANAGEMENT

- USING BLOCKCHAIN FOR QUALITY ASSURANCE AND PRODUCT STANDARDS
- TRACKING COMPLIANCE WITH REGULATORY STANDARDS
- BENEFITS FOR HIGH-VALUE OR REGULATED PRODUCTS

CHAPTER 13: BLOCKCHAIN FOR SUPPLIER COLLABORATION AND TRANSPARENCY

CHAPTER 14: REDUCING OPERATIONAL COSTS WITH BLOCKCHAIN

- COST-SAVING OPPORTUNITIES FROM AUTOMATED PROCESSES
- REDUCING INVENTORY SHRINKAGE AND STOCKOUTS
- EFFICIENCY GAINS IN INVENTORY REPLENISHMENT AND STOCK OPTIMIZATION

CHAPTER 15: CASE STUDIES: BLOCKCHAIN IN INVENTORY MANAGEMENT

- SUCCESS STORIES FROM VARIOUS INDUSTRIES (RETAIL, PHARMA, FOOD, MANUFACTURING)
- LESSONS LEARNED FROM IMPLEMENTING BLOCKCHAIN
- HOW EARLY ADOPTERS OVERCAME CHALLENGES

CHAPTER 16: BLOCKCHAIN'S ROLE IN REVERSE LOGISTICS AND RETURNS

- USING BLOCKCHAIN FOR EFFICIENT RETURNS MANAGEMENT
- ENSURING TRANSPARENCY IN PRODUCT RETURNS AND REFUNDS
- BENEFITS OF BLOCKCHAIN IN RECYCLING AND WASTE MANAGEMENT

CHAPTER 17: CHALLENGES AND LIMITATIONS OF BLOCKCHAIN IN INVENTORY MANAGEMENT

- TECHNICAL LIMITATIONS (SCALABILITY, SPEED, ENERGY CONSUMPTION)
- LEGAL AND REGULATORY HURDLES
- ORGANIZATIONAL CHALLENGES: SKILLS, COSTS, AND CULTURE CHANGE

CHAPTER 18: PRACTICAL GUIDE TO BLOCKCHAIN IMPLEMENTATION

- STEPS TO BEGIN BLOCKCHAIN ADOPTION IN INVENTORY SYSTEMS
- CHOOSING BLOCKCHAIN SERVICE PROVIDERS AND TECHNOLOGIES
- ROADMAP FOR SUCCESSFUL INTEGRATION AND LONG-TERM SUCCESS

CHAPTER 19: FUTURE TRENDS AND INNOVATIONS IN BLOCKCHAIN FOR INVENTORY

- BLOCKCHAIN AND AI FOR PREDICTIVE INVENTORY AND DEMAND PLANNING
- DAOS (DECENTRALIZED AUTONOMOUS ORGANIZATIONS) IN INVENTORY MANAGEMENT

- Future of Blockchain-based Inventory Financing and Tokenized Assets

CHAPTER 20: PREPARING FOR A BLOCKCHAIN-ENABLED INVENTORY FUTURE

- Embracing a Blockchain-driven Culture of Transparency and Accountability
- Strategic Foresight: Preparing for Technology Advancements
- Final Thoughts on Blockchain's Role in the Future of Inventory Management

Chapter 1: Introduction to Blockchain and Inventory Management

In recent years, blockchain technology has transcended its origins in cryptocurrency to emerge as a transformative force across multiple industries, including supply chain and inventory management. The fusion of blockchain with inventory systems introduces new possibilities for accuracy, transparency, and efficiency, making it a critical technology in today's complex and interconnected supply chains. This chapter will provide an introduction to blockchain technology, an overview of inventory management fundamentals, and an exploration of how blockchain is reshaping modern inventory systems. Additionally, it will delve into the key benefits blockchain offers for enhancing inventory control, accuracy, and transparency.

Basics of Blockchain Technology

Blockchain technology, often described as a "distributed ledger," is a decentralized database shared across a network of computers, known as nodes. Unlike traditional databases, where data is stored and managed by a central authority, blockchain allows data to be recorded in a way that is transparent, secure, and virtually tamper-proof. Each transaction or record (called a "block") is timestamped and linked to the previous block in the chain, creating an immutable, linear history of all entries.

Key features of blockchain include:

Decentralization: Unlike centralized systems, blockchain data is distributed across multiple nodes. This lack of a single point of control means that no one party has complete authority over the data, reducing the risk of manipulation or data loss.

Transparency: All participants in a blockchain network can view the ledger, promoting a high level of transparency. Although participants can see the data, sensitive information can be encrypted, ensuring privacy where necessary.

Security: Blockchain employs advanced cryptographic techniques to secure transactions. Once data is added to a blockchain, it is exceedingly difficult to alter, making blockchain inherently resistant to fraud and unauthorized access.

Immutability: Once a block is added to the blockchain, it cannot be changed or deleted. This immutability creates a permanent and unchangeable record of transactions.

Consensus Mechanisms: Blockchain networks rely on consensus mechanisms (such as Proof of Work or Proof of Stake) to validate and agree on the addition of new data. This ensures that all transactions are genuine and have been approved by the majority of participants.

Blockchain's decentralized, secure, and transparent nature provides a foundation for applications in industries that require secure, tamper-proof records. In inventory management, these characteristics translate to improved tracking, trust, and efficiency.

Inventory Management Overview

Inventory management is a crucial function in any organization that handles physical goods. It involves overseeing the storage, ordering, and control of stock to ensure a company can meet demand while minimizing excess inventory costs. Effective inventory management aims to balance inventory levels to prevent overstocking or stockouts, optimize cash flow, and ultimately enhance customer satisfaction.

Key functions in inventory management include:

Inventory Control: This involves keeping track of all inventory items and ensuring they are available when needed. Techniques such as stock rotation, periodic audits, and demand forecasting are essential to this process.

Inventory Accuracy: Accuracy is fundamental in inventory management. Organizations must know exactly how much stock they have, where it is located, and its condition. Miscounts or inaccurate records can lead to costly errors, such as stockouts or overstocking.

Order Management: This involves ensuring orders are placed at the right time to replenish stock without delay. Companies use reorder points, safety stock levels, and lead time calculations to optimize order timing.

Demand Forecasting: Accurate demand forecasting helps organizations anticipate how much inventory will be needed over a specific period. This is often achieved through analyzing historical sales data and considering seasonal trends or external factors.

Supply Chain Coordination: Inventory management doesn't happen in isolation; it is part of the larger supply chain ecosystem. Coordination with suppliers, transportation providers, and other supply chain partners is essential for efficient inventory flow.

Inventory management requires real-time visibility, accurate data, and coordinated actions across departments and locations. Traditional inventory systems rely on centralized databases, barcoding, and periodic audits, which often fall short in ensuring real-time accuracy and transparency. Blockchain offers a new way to meet these needs.

Importance of Blockchain in Modern Inventory Systems

As companies face mounting pressures for faster, more reliable deliveries, transparency, and accountability, blockchain has emerged as a valuable tool to modernize inventory management. Blockchain's decentralized, immutable, and transparent features address many challenges in traditional inventory systems, such as data inaccuracy, lack of trust between partners, and limited real-time visibility.

Real-Time Transparency and Visibility: Blockchain enables real-time visibility across the entire supply chain. All participants, including manufacturers, suppliers, and retailers, can view inventory levels and movement on a shared ledger. This transparency reduces delays, minimizes errors, and enables informed decision-making.

Enhanced Data Accuracy and Trust: Traditional inventory systems often suffer from data discrepancies due to manual entry errors, system silos, or delayed updates. Blockchain's distributed ledger ensures that all participants have access to a single source of truth, enhancing data accuracy and establishing trust.

Fraud Prevention and Security: Inventory fraud, such as manipulation of stock levels or unauthorized access to inventory records, poses significant risks. Blockchain's security mechanisms prevent unauthorized changes to records, significantly reducing the potential for fraud.

Improved Traceability: Traceability is crucial in industries where knowing the origin and journey of a product is essential (e.g., food, pharmaceuticals). Blockchain enables companies to trace products from their point of origin to their current location with absolute accuracy, which is vital for quality control and regulatory compliance.

Automation and Efficiency Gains: Blockchain enables smart contracts—self-executing contracts with terms directly written into code. Smart contracts automate processes such as reordering inventory when stock reaches a specific level, eliminating delays and reducing administrative burden.

Key Benefits for Inventory Control, Accuracy, and Transparency

Blockchain offers distinct advantages for inventory control, accuracy, and transparency, making it a valuable tool for modern inventory management. The following benefits outline how blockchain can transform these core inventory functions:

Enhanced Inventory Control: Blockchain provides precise, real-time tracking of inventory across all stages of the supply chain. With blockchain, inventory managers can monitor stock levels at different locations, track movement between warehouses, and receive alerts when items are shipped or received. This level of control allows companies to respond quickly to demand fluctuations and optimize stock levels, reducing the risk of stockouts or overstocking.

Increased Data Accuracy and Reduced Errors: In traditional systems, inventory data can be misreported due to human error, system silos, or delays in updating records. Blockchain's distributed ledger structure ensures that all data entries are verified, consistent, and immediately available to all stakeholders. This accuracy reduces costly errors, improves forecasting, and minimizes the need for manual audits.

Transparency Across the Supply Chain: Blockchain enables unparalleled transparency, as all stakeholders can view and verify inventory information in real time. This transparency is especially valuable for companies that work with multiple suppliers or operate in complex, global supply chains. When all parties can access the same data, it fosters trust and collaboration, streamlining inventory processes and enhancing relationships with suppliers and partners.

Improved Compliance and Traceability: Regulatory compliance and traceability are critical in industries like healthcare, food, and electronics, where companies must adhere to stringent safety and quality standards. Blockchain provides a complete, immutable record of a product's journey through the supply chain, ensuring that companies can verify compliance with regulations and address quality issues promptly if they arise.

Reduced Administrative Burden and Operational Efficiency: Blockchain can automate inventory management tasks, such as triggering reorders when stock reaches a specific threshold. Through smart contracts, blockchain reduces the need for manual intervention in routine processes, freeing up resources and improving operational efficiency. Additionally, the time and costs associated with reconciliation, auditing, and dispute resolution are significantly reduced, as all records are secure, accurate, and easily accessible.

Cost Savings: While implementing blockchain technology involves an initial investment, the long-term benefits often outweigh the costs. By reducing errors, enhancing efficiency, and minimizing fraud, blockchain can lead to significant cost savings. Better inventory control means less capital tied up in excess stock, and improved forecasting accuracy can reduce losses from stockouts or spoilage.

Flexibility and Scalability for Future Growth: As companies grow, they need inventory systems that can scale with them. Blockchain's modular, decentralized nature makes it highly adaptable to changing business needs, whether that involves expanding to new locations, introducing new product lines, or increasing order volume. Blockchain provides the flexibility to add or adjust data points, ensuring that inventory management practices remain relevant as the organization evolves.

In summary, blockchain technology addresses many of the challenges that traditional inventory management systems face, particularly in terms of control, accuracy, and transparency. As the digital economy continues to evolve, blockchain offers a robust, scalable solution for organizations aiming to modernize their inventory practices and improve their supply chain resilience. By integrating blockchain into inventory management, companies can enhance their operational efficiency, reduce costs, and foster stronger relationships with partners and customers through a transparent, trusted, and secure system.

The next chapter will explore how blockchain enables real-time inventory tracking, giving companies the ability to monitor and respond to changes with unprecedented speed and accuracy. With blockchain, inventory management is no longer a reactive process; it becomes a proactive, strategic component of business success.

Chapter 2: The Evolution of Blockchain in Supply Chains

- *Historical Development of Blockchain in Supply Chains*
- *Blockchain's Shift from Cryptocurrency to Inventory Applications*
- *Industry Drivers for Blockchain Adoption in Inventory Management*

Blockchain technology has quickly evolved from its original purpose as the foundation for cryptocurrencies to a transformative tool across industries, including supply chain and inventory management. As global supply chains grow in complexity and organizations demand greater transparency, accuracy, and security, blockchain has emerged as a solution for addressing some of the most challenging aspects of supply chain management. This chapter traces the historical development of blockchain in supply chains, explains its shift from cryptocurrency to inventory applications, and examines the industry drivers fueling its adoption in inventory management.

Historical Development of Blockchain in Supply Chains

Blockchain's origins can be traced back to 2008 with the release of Bitcoin, the first cryptocurrency powered by a decentralized, digital ledger. Bitcoin's blockchain introduced a novel way of storing and verifying transactions without relying on a central authority. This decentralized approach, which ensured transparency and security, quickly gained attention and led innovators to consider other applications for blockchain technology beyond cryptocurrency.

In the early 2010s, blockchain began to draw attention from industries that required transparent, tamper-proof record-keeping. Supply chain management, known for its complexity and interdependency, was a natural fit for blockchain's distributed ledger capabilities. For example, supply chains involve multiple stakeholders—including manufacturers, suppliers, logistics providers, retailers, and end customers—all of whom need reliable and synchronized information on product movements, conditions, and locations. Blockchain offered a potential solution by creating an immutable ledger that all participants could access, eliminating discrepancies and improving collaboration across the supply chain.

Around 2015, various industries started to experiment with blockchain in supply chain contexts, focusing primarily on traceability and transparency. This period saw the development of blockchain platforms and consortia focused on exploring its potential for tracking goods through supply chains. Projects were initiated in sectors like agriculture, pharmaceuticals, and luxury goods, where the ability to verify product origin, quality, and handling conditions was especially important.

Some early blockchain applications in supply chains include:

Food and Agriculture: Ensuring transparency about product origin and quality has long been a priority in the food industry. Blockchain provided a way to trace produce from farms to supermarkets, enabling companies to track each step and assure consumers of food safety. IBM's Food Trust blockchain network, developed with major retailers like Walmart, became a pioneering example in this field.

Pharmaceuticals: The pharmaceutical industry faces stringent requirements to verify product authenticity and prevent counterfeiting. Blockchain was introduced to track medications across the supply chain, ensuring they reach patients safely. Early initiatives, such as MediLedger, aimed to help pharmaceutical companies comply with regulatory standards for drug traceability.

Luxury Goods and Fashion: Counterfeiting and fraud are significant issues in luxury goods and fashion. Blockchain offered a means to verify the authenticity of high-value items by providing a permanent, unalterable record of each product's history. Early adopters, including Louis Vuitton and De Beers, leveraged blockchain to track the provenance of luxury items and precious gems.

As these applications developed, blockchain's potential in the supply chain became increasingly clear. Organizations recognized the advantages of a system that could provide reliable, real-time data across a complex web of stakeholders. By the late 2010s, more sectors were adopting blockchain to streamline supply chain processes, from inventory management to logistics and regulatory compliance.

Blockchain's Shift from Cryptocurrency to Inventory Applications

While blockchain technology was initially synonymous with cryptocurrency, its underlying features made it highly adaptable for other uses, particularly in supply chain and inventory management. The shift from blockchain as a cryptocurrency backbone to an inventory management tool represents a natural evolution in understanding and applying the technology's capabilities.

Several factors facilitated this shift:

Recognition of Blockchain's Distributed Ledger as an Asset for Transparency: Blockchain's decentralized structure, which prevents tampering and promotes transparency, was ideal for applications where trust and traceability were essential. In inventory management, knowing the precise location, condition, and history of goods is vital. Blockchain's distributed ledger provided a way to record and verify every step in the inventory lifecycle, ensuring accuracy and trust.

Growing Complexity of Global Supply Chains: As supply chains have become more globalized, inventory management has faced challenges due to the increased number of partners, varying regulatory requirements, and the demand for faster delivery times. Blockchain's ability to offer real-time, consistent data across borders and companies allowed inventory managers to streamline processes and improve efficiency in global operations.

Advances in Blockchain Technology: Initially, blockchain was limited by issues such as slow transaction speeds and high energy consumption. However, improvements in blockchain technology, including the development of more efficient consensus algorithms and hybrid blockchain models, made it a more viable option for enterprise applications. Newer blockchain platforms such as Ethereum and Hyperledger were designed to support smart contracts and scalable applications, paving the way for blockchain's use in areas like inventory management.

Integration with Other Technologies: Blockchain's integration with IoT and AI opened up new possibilities for inventory management. For instance, IoT devices, such as sensors and RFID tags, can automatically record inventory data, which blockchain can then securely store and share. AI, on the other hand, can analyze blockchain data to identify patterns, forecast demand, and optimize stock levels.

Shift in Regulatory Landscape: Regulatory bodies began to see blockchain's potential for improving supply chain traceability, particularly in industries with strict compliance standards, like pharmaceuticals, food, and aerospace. As governments and regulators encouraged greater transparency in supply chains, blockchain adoption became an attractive way for companies to meet these requirements.

These factors drove blockchain's transition from a cryptocurrency framework to a tool for optimizing inventory management. In this context, blockchain offers companies the ability to track inventory items across multiple stages, gain real-time insights, and streamline coordination among stakeholders.

Industry Drivers for Blockchain Adoption in Inventory Management

Several industry-specific trends and challenges have accelerated the adoption of blockchain in inventory management, making it a strategic tool for organizations seeking to optimize operations, reduce costs, and meet evolving customer expectations. These drivers include:

Demand for Real-Time Data: In today's fast-paced business environment, companies need real-time visibility into inventory levels and movements to respond to fluctuations in demand. Traditional systems often suffer from data lag and inaccuracies due to manual processes or isolated systems. Blockchain provides real-time, accurate data that is accessible to all stakeholders, enabling better decision-making and agile responses to market changes.

Need for Greater Transparency and Trust: Transparency has become a crucial requirement in modern supply chains, driven by consumer expectations, regulatory pressures, and the desire to build trust between supply chain partners. Blockchain's transparency fosters accountability, as all stakeholders can access the same verified information, reducing disputes, delays, and reliance on intermediaries.

Risk Mitigation and Fraud Prevention: Inventory fraud, counterfeiting, and theft are significant risks in supply chains. Blockchain's immutability and security features make it an effective solution for preventing unauthorized alterations to inventory records. By using blockchain, companies can significantly reduce risks associated with fraudulent activities and ensure the integrity of their data.

Supply Chain Resilience and Crisis Preparedness: Recent global events, such as the COVID-19 pandemic, have highlighted the need for resilient supply chains. Companies now recognize the importance of having systems that can quickly adapt to disruptions. Blockchain, with its secure, distributed nature, provides a level of resilience that helps companies maintain accurate, up-to-date inventory information even in the face of unexpected challenges.

Sustainability and Ethical Sourcing: Consumers and regulators are increasingly focused on the sustainability and ethical practices of supply chains. Blockchain enables companies to verify the origin and journey of raw materials, ensuring compliance with ethical sourcing and sustainability standards. For example, a company can use blockchain to track whether a product's raw materials were sourced responsibly, allowing them to make transparent claims about their supply chain practices.

Streamlining Compliance and Regulatory Requirements: Industries like pharmaceuticals, electronics, and food are subject to stringent regulatory requirements that mandate tracking and verifying the origin and handling of products. Blockchain's transparent and immutable ledger makes compliance easier by providing regulators and companies with an accurate, auditable record of each product's history. This is especially beneficial in regions with strict regulatory demands, where non-compliance can lead to costly penalties.

Cost Efficiency and Operational Optimization: Traditional inventory management systems require frequent audits, manual reconciliations, and coordination between multiple departments, which can be time-consuming and costly. Blockchain streamlines these processes by providing a unified, accurate record of inventory movements. This reduces the need for manual intervention, minimizes discrepancies, and ultimately leads to lower operational costs.

Enhanced Customer Satisfaction: In the digital age, customers expect fast, accurate, and transparent information about their orders. By leveraging blockchain, companies can offer end-to-end visibility into inventory and order status, enabling customers to track their purchases in real-time. Improved accuracy and transparency lead to higher customer satisfaction and foster brand loyalty.

In conclusion, blockchain technology has rapidly evolved from its cryptocurrency roots to become a valuable asset in supply chain and inventory management. Its ability to provide real-time transparency, security, and data accuracy addresses many challenges faced by traditional inventory systems. Industry-specific drivers, including the demand for transparency, the need to mitigate risk, and the push for cost efficiency, continue to propel blockchain adoption forward.

The next chapter will explore how blockchain enables real-time inventory tracking, giving companies unprecedented visibility and control over their inventory. By leveraging blockchain, businesses are better equipped to manage inventory, optimize operations, and stay competitive in an increasingly complex marketplace.

Chapter 3: Core Principles of Blockchain Technology

- *Decentralization, Immutability, and Transparency*
- *Types of Blockchains: Public, Private, and Consortium*
- *How Blockchain's Core Features Benefit Inventory Management*

Blockchain technology is built on core principles that make it a powerful tool for applications beyond its original role in cryptocurrency. These principles—decentralization, immutability, and transparency—are fundamental to the security, reliability, and trustworthiness that blockchain provides. Understanding these core principles and the types of blockchains available can help illustrate why blockchain is particularly well-suited to inventory management. In this chapter, we will explore these key principles, discuss the types of blockchains, and examine how each feature benefits inventory management.

Decentralization, Immutability, and Transparency

1. Decentralization

At the heart of blockchain technology is decentralization. Unlike traditional databases or information systems that rely on a centralized authority to maintain and validate data, blockchain operates through a distributed network of nodes. These nodes collectively verify and record data on the blockchain without the need for a central controller.

In a decentralized system, each participant has access to a shared ledger, and any changes must be agreed upon by the network. This setup reduces reliance on a single point of authority, mitigating risks associated with centralized systems, such as data breaches, manipulation, or single points of failure. Decentralization also creates a more secure and resilient network, as no single entity can control or alter the data without consensus from the network.

Benefits for Inventory Management: In inventory management, decentralization allows multiple stakeholders—such as suppliers, manufacturers, logistics providers, and retailers—to access the same information simultaneously. With everyone operating from a shared source of truth, discrepancies are minimized, and processes like stock checks, order processing, and product tracking become more efficient.

Decentralization also fosters trust, as no single party can alter inventory records without consensus.

2. Immutability

Immutability is the principle that once data is recorded on a blockchain, it cannot be altered or deleted. This is achieved through cryptographic hashing and consensus mechanisms that prevent any unauthorized modifications to the data. Every transaction or piece of information stored on the blockchain is given a unique hash, which serves as a fingerprint. Any alteration to the data would change the hash, making tampering immediately detectable. Additionally, as data is recorded in blocks linked chronologically to previous blocks, changing one block would require rewriting the entire blockchain—a near-impossible task in a decentralized network.

Benefits for Inventory Management: For inventory managers, immutability ensures that data related to inventory levels, product locations, and transaction histories is reliable and secure. With an immutable record, companies can track inventory through every stage of its journey, from manufacturing to delivery, without the risk of data being altered. This is particularly valuable in high-stakes industries like pharmaceuticals or food, where any modification could compromise product quality and safety. Immutability also simplifies auditing and compliance, as all data remains verifiable and intact.

3. Transparency

Transparency in blockchain refers to the ability for all participants in the network to view and verify the same data. Unlike traditional systems where data access is often limited to specific parties, blockchain allows authorized participants to view transaction histories in a secure and permissioned manner. This transparency promotes accountability among participants, as any changes are visible to the entire network.

In public blockchains, transparency is more extensive, allowing anyone to view transaction details, although they may not have direct control over the data. Private and consortium blockchains, on the other hand, provide controlled transparency, enabling organizations to share data with specific stakeholders while maintaining confidentiality.

Benefits for Inventory Management: Transparency is crucial in inventory management, as it fosters trust and cooperation among partners. With a transparent blockchain, supply chain partners can verify stock levels, track shipments, and monitor product conditions in real-time. This visibility enhances collaboration, minimizes misunderstandings, and reduces instances of stockouts, overstocking, or delays. For example, a retailer can check a supplier's inventory levels to forecast product availability accurately, while a logistics provider can update all parties on shipping status.

Types of Blockchains: Public, Private, and Consortium

Blockchain technology offers different structures to suit various needs. There are three main types of blockchains: public, private, and consortium. Each has unique features, advantages, and ideal applications within inventory management.

1. Public Blockchains

Public blockchains are open, permissionless networks that anyone can join, validate transactions on, and view. They are fully decentralized, allowing any participant to contribute to the network's operations, such as by mining (validating and adding transactions). Well-known examples of public blockchains include Bitcoin and Ethereum. In public blockchains, transparency and security are prioritized, and transactions are validated through mechanisms like proof of work or proof of stake, ensuring data integrity without central oversight.

Pros:

Complete decentralization and transparency.

Secure due to high levels of participation and cryptographic validation.

Accessible to anyone, making it ideal for applications that require wide-scale participation.

Cons:

Slower transaction speeds compared to private or consortium blockchains.

Higher energy consumption due to consensus algorithms like proof of work.

Potential for data privacy concerns as information is publicly accessible.

Use in Inventory Management: Public blockchains are less commonly used for inventory management, as many companies prioritize data privacy and efficiency. However, they may be useful in scenarios requiring broad transparency, such as verifying the authenticity of high-value items or tracking publicly traded commodities.

2. Private Blockchains

Private blockchains are restricted, permissioned networks where access is controlled by a central entity or group. Only approved participants can join, view data, and contribute to the ledger. Private blockchains provide more control over who can access and modify data, making them suitable for organizations that need privacy and faster transaction speeds.

Pros:

Controlled access and greater privacy.

Faster and more efficient transactions.

Better suited for internal processes within a single organization.

Cons:

Less decentralized than public blockchains.

Dependent on the trustworthiness of the controlling entity.

Use in Inventory Management: Private blockchains are ideal for organizations that want to manage their inventory in-house while maintaining data privacy. For example, a company can use a private blockchain to track internal inventory movements, automate stock replenishment, and monitor conditions without exposing data to external parties.

3. Consortium Blockchains

Consortium blockchains, also known as federated blockchains, are partially decentralized networks controlled by a group of organizations rather than a single entity. This type of blockchain provides the benefits of both public and private blockchains: it offers transparency and shared control without being fully open. Consortium blockchains are commonly used in industries where multiple organizations need to collaborate while maintaining control over their data.

Pros:

Shared control across multiple organizations, reducing reliance on a single authority.

Faster than public blockchains, with more transparency than private blockchains.

Ideal for collaborative applications requiring transparency and data sharing among trusted parties.

Cons:

More complex governance as multiple entities are involved.

Potential disagreements between consortium members on rules and policies.

Use in Inventory Management: Consortium blockchains are well-suited to supply chains and inventory management, where multiple stakeholders need access to shared data. For example, a consortium blockchain can help suppliers, manufacturers, and retailers synchronize inventory data, track products across borders, and verify delivery schedules. Consortium blockchains enhance transparency, reduce delays, and improve accountability among partners.

How Blockchain's Core Features Benefit Inventory Management

Blockchain's core principles—decentralization, immutability, and transparency—combined with its flexible structure, offer distinct advantages for inventory management:

Improved Data Accuracy: With blockchain, inventory data is recorded in a tamper-proof, secure ledger, ensuring accuracy and reducing the risk of data manipulation. This leads to better stock accuracy, reducing losses associated with shrinkage or human error.

Enhanced Traceability: Blockchain allows inventory managers to track products from their source to the end customer. This traceability is invaluable for managing recalls, verifying product authenticity, and meeting regulatory requirements.

Faster and More Efficient Transactions: Blockchain streamlines transaction processes, such as order confirmations, stock updates, and payments, by reducing reliance on intermediaries. Automated smart contracts can trigger actions when certain conditions are met, such as reordering inventory when stock levels fall below a set threshold.

Improved Collaboration Across Partners: Consortium blockchains create a shared, trusted network where multiple parties in the supply chain can access the same data in real time. This transparency improves collaboration, reduces bottlenecks, and increases operational efficiency.

Reduced Fraud and Shrinkage: Immutability ensures that no unauthorized changes are made to inventory records. This feature is particularly valuable in industries prone to counterfeiting, such as pharmaceuticals and luxury goods, where blockchain can verify product origin and authenticity.

In summary, the core principles of blockchain—decentralization, immutability, and transparency—provide the foundation for its transformative impact on inventory management. By selecting the appropriate type of blockchain, whether public, private, or consortium, organizations can address their unique needs for security, transparency, and efficiency. In the following chapters, we will delve deeper into specific blockchain applications and explore how they optimize various aspects of inventory management, from real-time tracking to demand forecasting.

Chapter 4: Current Challenges in Inventory Management

- *Issues in Traditional Inventory Systems (e.g., Fraud, Data Inaccuracy, Delays)*
- *Lack of Visibility and Accountability*
- *How Blockchain Can Address These Pain Points*

Effective inventory management is essential for maintaining optimal operations, meeting customer demand, and maximizing profitability. However, traditional inventory systems face numerous challenges that limit efficiency and accuracy, often resulting in lost revenue and strained business relationships. These issues include fraud, data inaccuracies, and operational delays, as well as a general lack of visibility and accountability throughout the supply chain. This chapter explores the pain points inherent in conventional inventory systems and examines how blockchain technology can help address these challenges.

Issues in Traditional Inventory Systems

Traditional inventory management systems often rely on centralized databases, manual data entry, and siloed information-sharing methods. These systems, while still widely used, have several vulnerabilities that affect inventory accuracy, increase costs, and impact customer satisfaction.

1. Fraud and Counterfeit Products

Fraud, including product counterfeiting and manipulation of inventory records, is a significant challenge for companies worldwide. Counterfeit goods lead to revenue losses, harm brand reputation, and, in some cases, endanger consumer safety. Fraud is especially problematic in industries like pharmaceuticals, luxury goods, and electronics, where counterfeiting is widespread. Traditional inventory systems struggle to prevent these issues because of limited traceability, lack of robust verification mechanisms, and the inability to validate the origins and movements of goods.

Example: In the pharmaceutical industry, counterfeit drugs are a major issue, as it's difficult to track the origins of products within traditional supply chain systems. This problem has life-threatening consequences for patients, damages public trust, and increases costs for companies that must work to recall and replace compromised products.

2. Data Inaccuracy and Human Error

Inventory management is highly dependent on accurate data. However, in traditional systems, data entry is often manual, leading to human error. Mistakes in recording stock levels, item locations, or product descriptions can quickly add up, causing inventory records to become inaccurate over time. Data inaccuracies result in miscounts, stockouts, overstocking, and even lost products. The reliance on paper records or outdated digital systems only exacerbates these challenges.

Example: A retail company relying on manual data entry could accidentally record incorrect quantities during stock audits. Over time, the inaccuracies accumulate, leading to incorrect reorder levels. This scenario often results in either excess inventory, tying up working capital, or stockouts, impacting customer satisfaction.

3. Operational Delays and Inefficiency

In traditional inventory systems, delays are common due to the dependence on manual processes and the involvement of intermediaries. Verifying product authenticity, checking stock levels, and reconciling data across departments or with external partners can take considerable time. These delays affect the entire supply chain, leading to longer lead times, delays in product delivery, and a lack of agility in responding to fluctuations in demand.

Example: A manufacturing company may face delays when waiting for parts to be delivered, leading to production bottlenecks. Without real-time data on parts availability, the company cannot adjust its production schedule efficiently, resulting in prolonged downtime.

Lack of Visibility and Accountability

Transparency and accountability are critical in inventory management, especially for companies dealing with complex supply chains. Traditional inventory systems, however, are often characterized by information silos and limited visibility. This lack of transparency and accountability can lead to several issues.

1. Siloed Information

Information silos are a major barrier to visibility in traditional inventory management systems. Different departments, such as procurement, warehousing, and logistics, may each maintain their own data, with limited real-time communication across the organization. This lack of coordination leads to duplicated records, miscommunication, and inefficient processes.

Example: A logistics team might not have visibility into inventory levels at the warehouse, leading to delays in shipping when an item is unexpectedly out of stock. Alternatively, sales and marketing may lack insights into available stock, affecting their ability to manage promotions effectively.

2. Limited Tracking Capabilities

Traditional inventory systems typically lack the tools needed to provide comprehensive, end-to-end tracking of goods. This shortfall limits a company's ability to trace products back to their origin or monitor them at every stage of the supply chain. When tracking is fragmented or inconsistent, it becomes challenging to verify product quality, trace product history, or hold specific parties accountable for delays or discrepancies.

Example: In the case of a product recall, a company using a traditional inventory system might struggle to trace the affected items back through the supply chain, resulting in delays and potential harm to consumers.

3. Challenges in Regulatory Compliance

Many industries, including healthcare, food, and electronics, are subject to strict regulatory standards that require accurate record-keeping and traceability. Traditional systems are often inadequate for ensuring full compliance with these regulations, as manual record-keeping and fragmented data can lead to missed compliance requirements, fines, or product recalls.

Example: A food distributor that lacks a streamlined tracking system may find it challenging to comply with food safety regulations, which often require detailed records of storage conditions, expiration dates, and shipment histories. Failing to maintain these records can result in regulatory penalties and loss of business reputation.

How Blockchain Can Address These Pain Points

Blockchain technology offers a unique solution to the problems found in traditional inventory management. By providing a decentralized, transparent, and secure ledger system, blockchain addresses these issues and enhances the efficiency and reliability of inventory systems.

1. Enhanced Security Against Fraud

Blockchain's decentralized and immutable structure makes it far more difficult for fraudulent activity to occur. Once data is entered into a blockchain, it is nearly impossible to alter without consensus from the network, ensuring that inventory records remain accurate and tamper-proof. Furthermore, blockchain can authenticate products by creating a verifiable chain of custody from the manufacturer to the consumer, reducing the risk of counterfeiting.

Example: In the electronics industry, blockchain can be used to verify the authenticity of products like smartphones or computer components. By recording each product's journey on an immutable blockchain, companies can provide customers with a secure and reliable way to confirm product authenticity.

2. Real-Time Data Accuracy

With blockchain, inventory data is recorded in real time and is accessible to all authorized parties. This setup eliminates the need for manual data entry and reduces the likelihood of human error, ensuring that inventory records are always up to date. Blockchain's smart contracts can automate data updates and trigger actions when specific conditions are met, such as reordering stock or updating stock levels.

Example: A warehouse can use blockchain to automate reordering based on real-time inventory levels. When stock for a particular item falls below a predetermined threshold, a smart contract on the blockchain can automatically initiate a purchase order, ensuring timely replenishment and preventing stockouts.

3. Increased Visibility and Traceability

Blockchain's transparency allows authorized participants to view and verify the same data, creating a single source of truth. This transparency enhances visibility across the supply chain, enabling companies to track inventory at each stage, from manufacturing to delivery. Improved visibility helps prevent issues such as overstocking or stockouts, reduces lead times, and enhances collaboration across supply chain partners.

Example: A retailer can use blockchain to gain visibility into a supplier's inventory, ensuring that stock is available before promotions are launched. This visibility helps avoid customer dissatisfaction due to backorders or delays.

4. Accountability Through Immutability

Blockchain's immutability ensures that data, once recorded, cannot be altered. This provides a high level of accountability among all parties involved in the supply chain. With blockchain, companies can maintain a verifiable record of inventory movements, reducing the risk of disputes and creating an audit trail that can be easily reviewed for compliance.

Example: In the event of a product recall, a food manufacturer can use blockchain to trace affected items back to the supplier, distributor, or storage facility, providing accountability and streamlining the recall process. This traceability not only minimizes the impact of the recall but also fosters trust with consumers.

5. Streamlined Compliance and Reporting

Blockchain's transparency and immutability make it an ideal tool for industries with regulatory requirements. By maintaining an immutable record of inventory transactions and conditions, companies can more easily meet regulatory standards, provide accurate records during audits, and respond more quickly to compliance issues.

Example: A pharmaceutical company can leverage blockchain to comply with regulatory requirements for tracking medication through the supply chain. With an immutable record of each transaction, the company can demonstrate compliance to regulators and ensure patient safety.

In conclusion, traditional inventory management systems face multiple challenges related to fraud, data accuracy, operational inefficiency, and limited visibility. Blockchain technology offers an effective solution to these issues, enabling secure, transparent, and efficient inventory management. By addressing the pain points of traditional systems, blockchain has the potential to transform inventory management and provide a more reliable, accurate, and accountable approach to managing stock across complex supply chains.

Chapter 5: Blockchain Architecture and Its Components

- *Key Components: Distributed Ledger, Blocks, Nodes, and Consensus Mechanisms*
- *Blockchain Data Storage and Access Models*
- *Smart Contracts: Enabling Automated Inventory Transactions*

Blockchain technology is a revolutionary architecture that underpins decentralized and transparent data exchange systems. For inventory management, blockchain's architecture provides a secure, tamper-resistant, and efficient framework, essential for building trust and reliability in the supply chain. This chapter will explore the critical components of blockchain architecture, including distributed ledgers, blocks, nodes, consensus mechanisms, data storage, access models, and smart contracts, all of which contribute to streamlined, automated inventory management.

Key Components of Blockchain Architecture

The blockchain architecture consists of several core components that work together to provide a decentralized and transparent system. Each element plays a specific role, enabling the blockchain to function effectively across multiple applications, including inventory management.

1. Distributed Ledger

The distributed ledger is the foundation of blockchain technology. Unlike traditional centralized databases, which rely on a single authority, a distributed ledger is shared across multiple participants (or nodes) in the network. Each participant maintains a copy of the entire ledger, ensuring that everyone has access to the same information in real time.

In inventory management, the distributed ledger allows all stakeholders — from suppliers to retailers — to access an accurate and up-to-date record of inventory data. This transparency reduces discrepancies, eliminates the need for intermediaries, and allows for instant data reconciliation across the network.

Example: A distributor and a retailer both have real-time access to the same inventory data on the blockchain. When goods are dispatched or received, the ledger is automatically updated for all parties, eliminating any confusion regarding stock levels.

2. Blocks

In a blockchain, data is organized into blocks, which are the fundamental building units of the ledger. Each block contains a batch of transactions and a unique identifier known as a "hash." Once a block is filled with data, it is sealed with a hash and added to the existing chain of blocks, forming an immutable chain of records.

In inventory management, each block can record various transactions, such as inventory movements, order confirmations, or stock level updates. Once added to the chain, this data cannot be altered, ensuring a secure and trustworthy record of inventory-related activities.

Example: A batch of newly manufactured products is added to inventory. The addition of these products is recorded in a block, including details such as item IDs, quantities, and timestamps. This information is then permanently linked to the inventory's history, creating a reliable audit trail.

3. Nodes

Nodes are individual computers or devices that participate in the blockchain network. Each node maintains a copy of the distributed ledger and validates transactions according to the network's consensus rules. Nodes can either be "full nodes," which store the complete blockchain, or "light nodes," which store only specific parts of it.

In inventory management, nodes can represent various stakeholders in the supply chain, such as suppliers, manufacturers, warehouses, and retailers. Each node can access and verify inventory information on the blockchain, enhancing data transparency and enabling faster, trust-based transactions.

Example: In a global supply chain, each warehouse operates as a node in the blockchain network. When inventory is moved from one warehouse to another, all nodes are updated, ensuring all stakeholders are aware of the stock location and quantity changes in real time.

4. Consensus Mechanisms

Consensus mechanisms are protocols used by nodes to validate and agree on transactions before adding them to the blockchain. Common consensus mechanisms include Proof of Work (PoW), Proof of Stake (PoS), and Practical Byzantine Fault Tolerance (PBFT). These mechanisms ensure that only legitimate transactions are recorded on the blockchain, providing an additional layer of security and trust.

For inventory management, consensus mechanisms help ensure that inventory data is accurate, up-to-date, and free from unauthorized modifications. By using a consensus protocol, companies can maintain high data integrity without relying on a centralized authority.

Example: When an inventory shipment is recorded, the nodes in the network reach a consensus to verify the shipment's authenticity. This consensus ensures that no fraudulent data can be entered into the blockchain, preventing unauthorized alterations.

Blockchain Data Storage and Access Models

Blockchain technology offers unique data storage and access models that are crucial for secure and efficient inventory management. The following features ensure that inventory data remains accessible, traceable, and secure.

1. Data Immutability

Data immutability is a core feature of blockchain, meaning that once data is entered into a block, it cannot be altered or deleted. This is achieved through cryptographic hashing and the chaining of blocks. Any attempt to alter a previous block would disrupt the entire chain, making it immediately noticeable.

In inventory management, immutability provides a tamper-proof record of all inventory movements and transactions. This is invaluable for audit trails, as companies can trace each inventory item's journey through the supply chain without the risk of data manipulation.

Example: If an error is found in an inventory count, a correction can only be made through a new transaction rather than altering past data. This new transaction is then added to the blockchain, preserving the history of changes and creating a reliable audit trail.

2. Access Control and Permissioned Blockchains

Access control is critical in ensuring that only authorized individuals can view or edit blockchain data. While some blockchains are public and allow anyone to join, permissioned blockchains are commonly used in inventory management. These blockchains restrict access to approved participants, ensuring that sensitive data remains secure and confidential.

In a permissioned blockchain for inventory management, companies can control who has access to inventory information. This is especially important for organizations that work with confidential data, such as pharmaceutical companies or high-value asset providers.

Example: A pharmaceutical company uses a permissioned blockchain to track drug inventory. Only authorized personnel, such as suppliers, quality controllers, and healthcare providers, have access to sensitive information about the origin and distribution of medications.

3. Scalability and Data Storage Solutions

Blockchain's data storage and scalability capabilities are essential for accommodating large amounts of data. For inventory management, this means that blockchains need to handle data from various transactions, product records, and updates. Layer-2 solutions and off-chain storage options are often used to improve scalability and efficiency.

Example: An e-commerce platform uses an off-chain storage solution to manage data-heavy images and detailed product descriptions. Only essential transactional information, such as product IDs and quantities, is stored directly on the blockchain to optimize speed and efficiency.

Smart Contracts: Enabling Automated Inventory Transactions

Smart contracts are self-executing contracts that automatically enforce the terms of an agreement when specific conditions are met. Written into code on the blockchain, these contracts can automate various tasks in inventory management, from restocking orders to issuing payments, without human intervention.

1. Automated Inventory Replenishment

One of the most significant applications of smart contracts in inventory management is automated replenishment. When inventory levels reach a certain threshold, a smart contract can trigger a reorder with the supplier, ensuring that stock levels are maintained without manual oversight.

Example: A retail store uses smart contracts to manage inventory. When the quantity of a specific item falls below a predefined threshold, the smart contract automatically places an order with the supplier. The entire process, including order confirmation and payment initiation, is completed without human intervention.

2. Streamlined Payment Processes

Smart contracts can also automate payment transactions between supply chain partners. Once an inventory shipment is delivered and verified on the blockchain, a smart contract can trigger an automatic payment from the buyer to the seller, eliminating the need for invoicing and reducing payment delays.

Example: A logistics provider delivers a shipment of goods, and the blockchain verifies delivery. A smart contract immediately releases the payment from the buyer's account to the logistics provider, ensuring a smooth and timely transaction.

3. Quality Control and Compliance Checks

Smart contracts can enforce quality control standards and compliance requirements. For instance, if an inventory item does not meet specified criteria (e.g., temperature control for perishable goods), the smart contract can automatically halt the transaction and initiate corrective actions.

Example: A food distributor uses smart contracts to monitor storage conditions for perishable products. If the temperature falls outside the acceptable range, the smart contract triggers an alert and prevents the affected items from being dispatched until the issue is resolved.

Understanding blockchain architecture and its core components is essential for harnessing the power of blockchain in inventory management. The distributed ledger provides transparency, blocks ensure data immutability, nodes facilitate collaboration, and consensus mechanisms guarantee accuracy and security. Furthermore, smart contracts automate crucial inventory processes, from restocking to payment, bringing unprecedented efficiency and reliability to inventory management.

With these foundational elements, companies can leverage blockchain to overcome traditional inventory challenges, paving the way for a more transparent, accountable, and efficient supply chain. As the following chapters will demonstrate, blockchain's transformative capabilities have only begun to reveal their potential in revolutionizing inventory management practices.

Chapter 6: Smart Contracts for Automated Inventory Management

- *Overview of Smart Contracts in Blockchain*
- *Benefits of Automation in Inventory Reordering and Stock Management*
- *Real-world Applications of Smart Contracts in Inventory Control*

Blockchain technology has introduced a new layer of transparency, security, and efficiency to many industries, including inventory management. A key innovation within blockchain that holds the potential to revolutionize inventory systems is the smart contract. Smart contracts are self-executing programs with the terms of the agreement directly written into code, enabling automated transactions when specific conditions are met. In inventory management, smart contracts can streamline reordering, payment processing, quality checks, and compliance, minimizing human intervention and reducing the risk of errors.

In this chapter, we'll explore the fundamentals of smart contracts, their advantages in automating inventory processes, and real-world applications where smart contracts are already proving invaluable in inventory control.

Overview of Smart Contracts in Blockchain

Smart contracts are protocols that operate on blockchain networks, designed to automatically enforce the terms of an agreement without requiring a central authority or intermediary. Originally conceptualized by computer scientist Nick Szabo in the 1990s, the modern application of smart contracts on blockchain began with the Ethereum blockchain, which allows for programmable, automated contracts. These contracts are decentralized, secure, and immutable, making them ideal for industries like supply chain and inventory management where accuracy, trust, and traceability are critical.

A smart contract operates based on a simple "if/then" structure. For example, "if inventory falls below a certain threshold, then reorder stock." In the context of inventory management, these self-executing contracts can handle a range of tasks, such as automatically placing restocking orders when levels reach a predefined minimum or releasing payments once products are received and verified.

Example of a Basic Smart Contract: Let's say a retailer has a smart contract with a supplier to replenish stock when it drops below 50 units. The smart contract is coded as follows:

Condition: Inventory reaches less than 50 units.

Action: An automatic order is placed with the supplier for 100 units.

Outcome: Once the supplier delivers the order, the smart contract verifies the delivery and processes payment.

This level of automation can have a transformative effect on inventory management by enhancing speed, accuracy, and accountability.

Benefits of Automation in Inventory Reordering and Stock Management

Automation through smart contracts offers numerous benefits for inventory management, particularly in improving efficiency, accuracy, and cost-effectiveness. Some of the primary advantages include:

1. Reduced Human Error and Enhanced Accuracy

Manual processes are often error-prone, particularly when managing large inventories across multiple locations. Errors in stock data can lead to overstocking, understocking, and inefficiencies that directly impact the bottom line. Smart contracts automate processes such as reordering, ensuring that actions are taken only when specific conditions are met, thereby reducing errors and improving the reliability of inventory data.

Example: A company has historically experienced issues with inventory data due to manual errors. By implementing smart contracts to automate stock updates, the company reduces discrepancies and achieves a more accurate, real-time view of inventory levels.

2. Improved Efficiency and Cost Savings

Automating inventory processes with smart contracts can lead to significant cost savings by minimizing the need for manual intervention and reducing delays in inventory-related tasks. Since smart contracts can execute actions instantly when conditions are met, tasks that might take days to process manually — such as reordering or payment approvals — can be completed in seconds.

Example: A distributor uses smart contracts to handle reorders for fast-moving products. As soon as inventory falls below a certain level, an order is triggered and sent to the supplier. This automation eliminates the need for staff to manually monitor stock levels, freeing up time and resources for more strategic activities.

3. Enhanced Transparency and Traceability

Blockchain's transparency means that every transaction and process executed by a smart contract is permanently recorded and visible to authorized stakeholders. This transparency allows all parties to track and verify inventory movements, leading to improved trust and accountability across the supply chain.

Example: A food manufacturer utilizes smart contracts to track shipments of perishable goods. Each stage of the inventory journey — from supplier to distributor to retailer — is recorded on the blockchain, allowing every stakeholder to see when and where the goods were last handled.

4. Streamlined Compliance and Quality Control

Smart contracts can enforce quality control and compliance standards by setting criteria that must be met before proceeding with a transaction. For instance, a smart contract might be programmed to reject shipments if a product doesn't meet specific temperature requirements. This can be especially useful in industries like pharmaceuticals or food, where regulatory compliance is strict.

Example: A pharmaceutical company requires specific temperature conditions for its drug shipments. A smart contract embedded with compliance parameters automatically rejects shipments if temperature readings fall outside the acceptable range, ensuring product quality and regulatory compliance.

5. Real-Time Data and Inventory Optimization

With smart contracts, businesses can achieve real-time inventory data, providing insights into stock levels, order statuses, and demand patterns. This real-time data can help optimize inventory levels, reducing holding costs and avoiding stockouts.

Example: An e-commerce company uses smart contracts to manage its warehouse inventory. The smart contract system provides real-time data on which products are nearing low stock levels, allowing the company to reorder before stockouts occur.

Real-World Applications of Smart Contracts in Inventory Control

Smart contracts are already being implemented in various industries to solve specific challenges in inventory management. Here are some real-world applications that demonstrate the versatility and impact of smart contracts in automating inventory control:

1. Automated Inventory Reordering

One of the most common uses of smart contracts in inventory management is automating the reordering process. For companies with high inventory turnover, maintaining optimal stock levels can be challenging and time-consuming. By setting predefined thresholds, companies can ensure that reordering is triggered automatically, preventing stockouts and minimizing inventory holding costs.

Case Study: A retail chain employs smart contracts to manage inventory across multiple stores. Each store's stock levels are monitored in real-time, and as soon as the quantity of an item falls below a preset threshold, the smart contract automatically places an order with the supplier. This automation helps the retailer prevent stockouts, particularly during high-demand seasons.

2. Payment Automation for Inventory Purchases

Smart contracts can streamline the payment process by automating payments once specific conditions are met, such as verifying the receipt of goods. This can eliminate the time lag associated with traditional invoicing and payment methods, reduce the risk of payment delays, and enhance supplier relationships.

Case Study: A manufacturing company uses smart contracts to automate payments to its raw material suppliers. Once the goods are delivered and verified through the blockchain, the smart contract releases the payment, significantly speeding up the procurement cycle and improving cash flow management.

3. Quality Control for Sensitive Inventory

Industries dealing with perishable or sensitive goods — such as pharmaceuticals, food, or chemicals — require stringent quality control measures. Smart contracts can enforce these measures by embedding specific quality criteria within the contract itself. If a shipment does not meet these criteria, the smart contract can automatically trigger a response, such as holding the shipment for further inspection.

Case Study: A food distribution company uses smart contracts to monitor temperature-sensitive items during transit. Each shipment is equipped with IoT sensors that track temperature data and feed it to the blockchain. If the temperature deviates from acceptable levels, the smart contract immediately alerts the company and puts the shipment on hold, ensuring product safety.

4. Supplier Performance Management

Smart contracts can also help monitor supplier performance by tracking metrics such as delivery timeliness, quality of goods, and adherence to contractual terms. Performance data recorded on the blockchain provides a clear, immutable record that can be used for supplier evaluations and decision-making.

Case Study: A global electronics company uses smart contracts to track supplier performance. The contract logs delivery times, the condition of goods received, and adherence to quality standards. Suppliers with a history of delays or quality issues are flagged, enabling the company to make data-driven decisions regarding future partnerships.

5. Inventory Tracking and Authentication in Luxury Goods

For industries that deal with high-value items, such as luxury goods, counterfeiting and unauthorized sales can be a significant problem. Smart contracts, combined with blockchain's traceability, can authenticate the origin and ownership of these items, allowing for more secure and reliable inventory tracking.

Case Study: A luxury fashion brand implements blockchain to authenticate its products. Each item is assigned a unique digital ID recorded on the blockchain. When an item changes hands (e.g., from manufacturer to distributor to retailer), the transaction is recorded by a smart contract, allowing consumers to verify the product's authenticity and origin.

Smart contracts represent a powerful tool for automated inventory management, offering unprecedented levels of efficiency, accuracy, and transparency. By automating routine tasks such as reordering, payment processing, and quality control, smart contracts reduce human intervention, lower operational costs, and mitigate risks associated with manual processes. They also provide real-time insights into inventory data, enabling companies to make informed, data-driven decisions that enhance their overall supply chain resilience.

In real-world applications, smart contracts are already proving their value in automating reordering processes, enforcing quality standards, and ensuring prompt payment to suppliers. As blockchain technology and smart contracts continue to evolve, we can expect to see even more sophisticated applications emerge, further transforming the landscape of inventory management. With the potential to eliminate inefficiencies and create a more transparent, reliable supply chain, smart contracts are poised to become a critical component of inventory management in the digital era.

Chapter 7: Digital Tokens and Asset Management in Inventory

- *Understanding Tokens as Inventory Units*
- *Digital Representation of Inventory Assets on Blockchain*
- *Using Tokenization for Better Asset Tracking and Management*

Blockchain has introduced new ways to manage and track assets through the concept of digital tokens, transforming how inventory assets are represented, tracked, and managed. Digital tokens can serve as unique, verifiable representations of inventory units, enabling businesses to digitize physical inventory items and facilitate seamless tracking, transparency, and accountability. Tokenization not only improves asset management but also helps streamline operations, reduce fraud, and enhance data accuracy.

In this chapter, we'll explore how tokens work as inventory units, how digital representation on blockchain benefits inventory systems, and how tokenization can enhance asset tracking and management.

Understanding Tokens as Inventory Units

In the realm of blockchain, a "token" is a digital representation of an asset or unit of value. Initially developed to represent cryptocurrencies, tokens have evolved to represent a wide range of physical and digital assets. In inventory management, tokens can act as digital equivalents of individual items or units of inventory, allowing businesses to monitor and manage these items with greater precision and efficiency.

Types of Tokens in Blockchain: Tokens generally fall into two main categories:

Fungible Tokens: These are interchangeable and identical, much like currency. Each unit has the same value and characteristics as another unit. For example, a warehouse could tokenize a batch of identical products with fungible tokens, making it easy to track quantities rather than individual items.

Non-Fungible Tokens (NFTs): These are unique, with each token representing a specific, distinguishable asset. NFTs can be particularly useful in managing unique inventory items or high-value assets, where it's essential to track individual units with unique characteristics.

Using Tokens as Inventory Units: In a blockchain-based inventory system, each item or batch of inventory can be assigned a token. This token acts as a digital certificate, storing essential information about the item, such as:

Product details: SKU, type, and description.

Quantity and batch information: Units per batch, batch ID, and expiration date.

Origin and ownership: Manufacturing details, current location, and chain of custody.

Tokenizing inventory allows businesses to gain a real-time, immutable record of each item's status, location, and history. Every time the inventory changes hands — from supplier to distributor, for instance — the associated token is updated on the blockchain, creating a reliable and transparent record.

Digital Representation of Inventory Assets on Blockchain

Digitizing inventory assets through tokens allows businesses to manage physical goods with unprecedented accuracy. Blockchain technology provides a secure, decentralized system where these digital assets (or tokens) can be tracked, verified, and managed transparently.

Benefits of Digital Representation:

Transparency and Traceability: Blockchain's immutable ledger allows authorized stakeholders to trace the history of an asset, from manufacturing to delivery. Every transaction or movement is recorded in real-time, providing a transparent view of inventory.

Security and Accountability: Each tokenized asset is permanently recorded on the blockchain, reducing opportunities for fraud and theft. Only authorized users can access or modify information, ensuring data integrity.

Reduction in Discrepancies: Traditional inventory systems can often suffer from data inaccuracies and discrepancies due to manual entries and human error. Blockchain tokenization minimizes these issues by creating a single source of truth for all inventory-related data.

Example of Tokenized Inventory Tracking: Consider a pharmaceutical company managing temperature-sensitive drugs. Each batch of medication is assigned a digital token on the blockchain. As the drugs move from manufacturer to distributor and then to the pharmacy, each change in location and temperature reading is recorded through the token. This level of traceability ensures compliance with regulatory standards and provides a clear, auditable trail for each batch.

Digital Twin Concept: Tokenization enables the concept of a "digital twin" — a virtual model of a physical asset. A digital twin is continuously updated to reflect the current status of its real-world counterpart. For instance, if a pallet of goods is damaged in transit, the digital twin reflects this issue, helping the company take swift corrective action.

Using Tokenization for Better Asset Tracking and Management

Tokenization offers an array of advantages for inventory asset management, enabling more accurate tracking, improved accountability, and streamlined processes. Here's how tokenization can optimize asset tracking and management in practical terms:

1. Enhanced Asset Visibility

Tokenization provides real-time visibility into inventory, allowing businesses to monitor the movement, condition, and location of assets continuously. This level of visibility is particularly beneficial for managing large inventories spread across multiple locations, as it reduces the risk of items being misplaced, delayed, or miscounted.

Example: A retail chain with stores across different regions uses tokenized inventory to track stock levels in real-time. Each item is assigned a digital token, and as products move through the supply chain, their tokens are updated. This allows the retailer to identify low-stock areas and optimize inventory distribution across all locations.

2. Efficient Reconciliation and Auditing

Traditional inventory audits can be time-consuming and costly. Tokenization simplifies reconciliation and auditing by maintaining an accurate, up-to-date record of all inventory transactions. Auditors can access a complete, transparent history of each asset, making it easier to verify data and identify any irregularities.

Example: An electronics distributor performs quarterly audits using tokenized data. Since each item's movement is recorded on the blockchain, auditors can verify inventory counts and locations with minimal manual effort. This approach reduces the time required for audits and enhances data accuracy.

3. Improved Demand Planning and Forecasting

Tokenization enables businesses to analyze inventory data in real-time, providing valuable insights into demand patterns and seasonal trends.

These insights allow businesses to make better-informed decisions about reordering, stocking, and production, reducing the likelihood of overstocking or stockouts.

Example: A food and beverage company uses tokenized inventory data to monitor product demand. By analyzing the frequency and timing of tokenized transactions, the company identifies which products have higher turnover and adjusts its production schedule accordingly. This proactive approach helps the company meet demand while minimizing excess inventory.

4. Reduction of Inventory Shrinkage and Loss

Inventory shrinkage, due to theft, damage, or administrative errors, can significantly impact a company's profitability. Tokenization addresses these challenges by creating a secure, verifiable record of each asset's status and movements, reducing opportunities for shrinkage.

Example: A high-end jewelry retailer uses tokenization to track valuable items from the supplier to the retail store. Each piece of jewelry is represented by a non-fungible token on the blockchain, allowing the company to verify its location and condition at every stage. This transparency reduces the risk of loss or theft and builds customer trust in product authenticity.

5. Automated Compliance and Regulatory Reporting

Tokenization simplifies regulatory compliance by creating an accurate, traceable record of each asset's history. For industries with strict regulations, such as pharmaceuticals or food, blockchain tokenization allows companies to provide proof of compliance quickly and efficiently.

Example: A pharmaceutical distributor uses tokenized inventory data to meet regulatory requirements. When regulators request proof of drug handling and storage conditions, the distributor provides a complete, blockchain-verified record for each batch, simplifying the audit process and demonstrating compliance.

Digital tokens have transformed how companies manage and track inventory assets, offering greater transparency, accountability, and efficiency. By assigning tokens to inventory items, businesses can monitor stock levels, streamline processes, and reduce errors, resulting in a more agile and resilient supply chain.

Tokenization creates a digital representation of physical assets, allowing companies to track and manage inventory in real-time and gain deep insights into asset performance and demand trends. From enhanced asset visibility to automated compliance reporting, tokenization provides a comprehensive solution for the challenges of modern inventory management.

As blockchain technology continues to evolve, tokenization's role in inventory management is likely to expand, with new applications emerging to further enhance operational efficiency, data accuracy, and supply chain resilience. Embracing tokenization can enable companies to stay competitive in an increasingly complex and dynamic marketplace, where precision, speed, and transparency are paramount.

Chapter 8: Inventory Tracking and Traceability with Blockchain

- *Real-time Tracking Across the Supply Chain*
- *Blockchain's Role in Ensuring Traceability and Authenticity*
- *Benefits of Traceability for Product Recalls and Quality Assurance*

Inventory tracking and traceability are crucial for managing a supply chain efficiently, ensuring product quality, and building consumer trust. Traditional inventory systems often lack the tools needed for accurate, real-time tracking across various supply chain stages, leading to issues like delayed shipments, misplaced inventory, and reduced accountability. Blockchain technology offers a robust solution by enabling real-time tracking, ensuring traceability, and verifying authenticity at every stage. Through this chapter, we'll explore how blockchain enhances inventory tracking, the role it plays in traceability and product authenticity, and the benefits for product recalls and quality assurance.

Real-time Tracking Across the Supply Chain

In traditional inventory systems, tracking products through the supply chain can be a time-consuming and complex process, often relying on data silos, multiple handoffs, and limited visibility into each transaction. Blockchain's decentralized, transparent ledger offers a solution to these challenges, allowing every participant in the supply chain — from suppliers to manufacturers, distributors, and retailers — to access a shared, single source of truth in real time.

How Blockchain Enables Real-time Tracking:

Decentralized Ledger: Blockchain's decentralized ledger allows all authorized participants to access the same information at any time, making it easy to track an item's location and status in real-time.

Immutable Transactions: Each transaction, such as a transfer of goods or a change in inventory location, is permanently recorded on the blockchain, creating a reliable history of each item's journey through the supply chain.

Automated Updates: Using IoT devices integrated with blockchain, physical items can update their blockchain status automatically. For instance, if a product moves from a warehouse to a retail store, the IoT sensor can trigger an automatic update to the blockchain.

Benefits of Real-time Tracking with Blockchain:

Enhanced Visibility: All parties involved in the supply chain can monitor product movements in real time, reducing the chances of items getting lost or misplaced.

Faster Response to Issues: Real-time tracking allows companies to quickly identify bottlenecks, delays, or anomalies and respond promptly.

Improved Demand Planning: With real-time inventory data, companies can make informed decisions about stock levels, restocking needs, and order fulfillment strategies.

Example: A global electronics company uses blockchain for real-time inventory tracking. As each shipment moves from one stage to the next, it is scanned, and an entry is automatically added to the blockchain. This level of visibility allows the company to monitor inventory levels globally, minimizing stockouts and preventing overstocking.

Blockchain's Role in Ensuring Traceability and Authenticity

Traceability and authenticity are essential for industries like food, pharmaceuticals, and luxury goods, where product quality and safety directly impact consumer trust and compliance with regulatory standards. Blockchain's immutable ledger and decentralized structure create a transparent, tamper-proof record of every step in the supply chain, ensuring that products are traceable and verifiable from origin to the end consumer.

How Blockchain Ensures Traceability:

Immutable Record of Each Transaction: Every time an item moves along the supply chain, blockchain records this transaction permanently. This record is accessible to all participants, making it easy to trace the item's journey.

Unique Digital Identity for Each Item: Blockchain allows each inventory item to have a unique digital identifier, which represents its batch number, origin, manufacturing details, and transportation history.

Chain of Custody: Blockchain helps establish a clear chain of custody, showing every party involved in handling the product. This chain of custody enhances accountability, making it harder for counterfeit or unauthorized goods to enter the supply chain.

Authenticity Verification with Blockchain:

Eliminating Counterfeit Products: Each item's digital record on the blockchain provides a tamper-proof way to verify its authenticity, making it easier to detect and prevent counterfeiting.

Enhanced Consumer Trust: When consumers know that a product's history is verifiable through blockchain, they're more likely to trust its authenticity, especially in industries such as luxury goods and pharmaceuticals.

Example: A luxury watch manufacturer integrates blockchain to combat counterfeit products. Each watch is assigned a unique blockchain identifier upon manufacturing, recording every detail from production to retail. When a customer purchases the watch, they can scan a QR code linked to the blockchain, verifying its authenticity and origin.

Benefits of Traceability for Product Recalls and Quality Assurance

Blockchain's traceability features are invaluable for product recalls and quality assurance, providing rapid and precise identification of affected products. In traditional inventory systems, identifying the exact batch, location, and recipient of defective products can be complex and time-consuming, leading to higher recall costs and increased risks to consumer safety. Blockchain streamlines the process, reducing response times and improving safety standards.

Product Recalls with Blockchain:

Accurate Identification of Affected Products: Blockchain's detailed record-keeping makes it easy to identify the exact batches and locations of products involved in a recall, preventing the need to pull unaffected products.

Efficient Communication with Stakeholders: With real-time tracking, blockchain allows all stakeholders to be immediately informed of a recall, speeding up the process and reducing potential harm to consumers.

Minimizing Recall Costs: By accurately identifying affected products, companies can recall only those items, reducing the financial and environmental impact of recalls.

Example: A food manufacturer discovers contamination in a batch of dairy products. Using blockchain's traceability features, the company identifies the specific batches and locations affected and initiates a targeted recall, informing retailers and distributors within hours. This precision minimizes waste and ensures consumer safety.

Quality Assurance Benefits:

Continuous Monitoring of Quality Standards: Blockchain allows for consistent monitoring of quality parameters, such as storage temperature or handling conditions, which are recorded on the blockchain for each item.

Real-time Quality Alerts: When blockchain is integrated with IoT, sensors can automatically record quality-related data, such as temperature changes. If the temperature exceeds acceptable limits, a blockchain entry is created, and an alert is sent to relevant parties.

Improved Regulatory Compliance: Industries with stringent regulatory standards, like pharmaceuticals, can use blockchain to prove compliance by providing authorities with a tamper-proof record of every quality check along the supply chain.

Example: A pharmaceutical company uses IoT-enabled sensors to monitor the temperature of vaccines during transportation. Each time the temperature falls outside the acceptable range, an entry is automatically logged on the blockchain. This data allows the company to ensure compliance and prevent the distribution of compromised products.

The ability to track and trace inventory in real-time is a transformative feature of blockchain technology, offering a robust solution to some of the longstanding challenges in inventory management. Blockchain provides a transparent, secure, and reliable method for tracking inventory throughout the supply chain, from origin to consumer, enhancing visibility, reducing errors, and improving accountability. For industries where product authenticity, quality assurance, and regulatory compliance are paramount, blockchain's traceability features offer a competitive advantage.

Blockchain's real-time tracking capabilities also empower companies to respond quickly to recalls, optimize demand planning, and deliver better customer experiences. By embracing blockchain, organizations can elevate their inventory management practices to a new level of precision and reliability, ensuring that their supply chains are agile, transparent, and trustworthy.

This shift toward blockchain-based inventory tracking is not just a trend but a necessary step in modernizing supply chains for a rapidly evolving global marketplace. As more industries adopt blockchain, its role in ensuring traceability and authenticity in inventory management will continue to grow, setting a new standard for supply chain excellence and accountability.

Chapter 9: Blockchain and IoT Integration for Inventory Management

- *Role of IoT Devices in Collecting Inventory Data*
- *IoT Sensors and Blockchain for Real-time Monitoring*
- *Case Examples of Blockchain-IoT Integrated Inventory Systems*

The integration of blockchain and the Internet of Things (IoT) is revolutionizing inventory management. IoT devices, including sensors, trackers, and smart devices, play a critical role in collecting real-time data on inventory, from location and condition to environmental factors like temperature and humidity. When combined with blockchain, this data becomes securely stored, tamper-proof, and accessible to all relevant stakeholders in the supply chain. In this chapter, we'll explore the role of IoT in collecting inventory data, how blockchain and IoT work together for real-time monitoring, and real-world examples of this powerful integration in action.

Role of IoT Devices in Collecting Inventory Data

IoT devices are essentially smart sensors or connected devices that can monitor, collect, and share data in real time. They are increasingly used in inventory management for a variety of purposes, such as tracking product location, monitoring environmental conditions, and detecting product movements. By automatically gathering and transmitting data, IoT devices remove much of the manual work involved in tracking inventory, reduce human error, and provide a level of detail and accuracy previously unattainable.

Types of IoT Devices Used in Inventory Management:

RFID Tags and GPS Trackers: These devices are widely used to track product location and movements. They allow companies to know the exact position of an item within a warehouse or during transportation, helping to optimize logistics and reduce lost or misplaced inventory.

Environmental Sensors: IoT devices equipped with sensors can monitor critical factors like temperature, humidity, and light exposure, which is crucial for perishable goods, pharmaceuticals, and electronics.

Weight Sensors and Load Cells: These devices help monitor stock levels by measuring the weight of products or materials. This data enables automatic updates on inventory status and alerts when levels fall below a specified threshold.

Smart Shelves and Bins: These IoT-enabled storage solutions can detect when items are added or removed, providing real-time updates on stock levels and helping prevent stockouts or overstocking.

Benefits of IoT for Inventory Management:

Real-time Data Collection: IoT devices provide continuous, real-time updates on inventory status, allowing for precise tracking and faster response times.

Automated Inventory Updates: By collecting and transmitting data automatically, IoT reduces the need for manual data entry, minimizing errors and streamlining processes.

Enhanced Data Accuracy: IoT devices capture precise data, reducing discrepancies and improving decision-making with more reliable information.

Example: A global retailer uses RFID tags and GPS-enabled trackers to monitor the location of their products at every point in the supply chain. This system ensures accurate and timely information about product availability, minimizing stockouts and enhancing delivery efficiency.

IoT Sensors and Blockchain for Real-time Monitoring

When IoT devices are integrated with blockchain, the data they collect is automatically recorded onto the blockchain, where it becomes part of a secure, immutable ledger accessible to all stakeholders in the supply chain. This combination is particularly powerful because it adds transparency and trust to IoT-collected data, addressing common concerns about data integrity and security.

How Blockchain Enhances IoT Monitoring:

Immutable Data Storage: The data collected by IoT devices is recorded on the blockchain, creating a permanent, unchangeable record of every transaction or update. This makes it impossible to alter historical data, which is crucial for audits, compliance, and accountability.

Decentralized Access: With blockchain, all authorized parties in the supply chain have real-time access to the same data, reducing the chances of miscommunication or information silos.

Automated Verification: Blockchain can automate the verification of data provided by IoT devices, ensuring that only accurate and validated information is shared with supply chain partners.

Applications of IoT-Blockchain Integration in Real-time Monitoring:

Condition Monitoring: IoT sensors embedded in packaging can monitor temperature, humidity, and other conditions. For instance, in pharmaceutical or food supply chains, IoT devices track the conditions of products and automatically log any deviation onto the blockchain. This ensures that products are handled within required conditions and allows for quick corrective action if any issue arises.

Inventory Movement Tracking: IoT devices track the movement of inventory through various points in the supply chain. Blockchain records each location update, creating a tamper-proof record of the item's journey. This helps prevent issues like theft, misplacement, or counterfeiting.

Stock Level Monitoring: Smart shelves and bins integrated with IoT sensors can monitor stock levels continuously. Whenever inventory is low, the system can automatically trigger a restocking request or alert relevant staff. Blockchain records these transactions, providing a transparent history of inventory levels and replenishments.

Example: A global logistics company leverages IoT sensors to track the temperature of perishable goods in transit. Each time the temperature changes beyond a specified threshold, the sensor triggers an automatic update that is recorded on the blockchain. This real-time data helps maintain product quality and allows for immediate action if any issues arise.

Case Examples of Blockchain-IoT Integrated Inventory Systems

The combined power of IoT and blockchain is being harnessed by various industries to streamline and secure inventory management, ensure product quality, and enhance transparency. Let's look at some real-world case examples where companies have successfully implemented blockchain-IoT integrated inventory systems.

1. Pharmaceutical Supply Chain Management: In the pharmaceutical industry, the storage and transportation of drugs require strict adherence to specific conditions, such as temperature control. A major pharmaceutical company has implemented an IoT-blockchain solution to track the movement and condition of its drugs from manufacturing to distribution. IoT sensors placed in shipping containers monitor the temperature and humidity in real time, while each update is recorded on the blockchain. If a deviation is detected, it is instantly logged and sent to relevant stakeholders, allowing for corrective action. The blockchain record also helps in auditing and ensures compliance with regulatory standards, as every data point is permanently stored.

2. Luxury Goods Authentication: A luxury goods manufacturer uses blockchain and IoT to combat counterfeiting. Each item is tagged with an RFID chip that contains a unique ID tied to a blockchain record. As the item moves through the supply chain, the RFID chip is scanned at various checkpoints, updating its blockchain record. This creates a secure and immutable trail of provenance, enabling customers to verify authenticity when they purchase the product. The integration of IoT and blockchain thus builds trust with consumers by guaranteeing that the product is genuine.

3. Food Supply Chain Traceability: A grocery retailer partners with suppliers to use IoT and blockchain technology to track the origin and condition of perishable items like fruits, vegetables, and seafood. IoT sensors monitor storage temperatures, while blockchain stores data on the entire supply chain journey. In the event of a contamination issue, the retailer can quickly trace the affected batch back to its source, minimizing the scope of recalls and ensuring customer safety. This integration provides end-to-end traceability, allowing the retailer to respond swiftly and responsibly to any quality issues.

4. Automotive Parts Management: An auto manufacturer uses IoT and blockchain to monitor and trace parts throughout its supply chain. RFID and GPS-enabled trackers monitor the movement and location of each part, while blockchain records every handoff. In case of a recall, the company can quickly trace defective parts to specific vehicles or suppliers, reducing the time and cost associated with recalls. The transparency and accountability provided by blockchain enhance supply chain reliability and reduce operational risks.

The integration of IoT and blockchain is transforming inventory management by making real-time monitoring more accurate, secure, and transparent. IoT devices act as a bridge between the physical and digital worlds, continuously collecting data about inventory status, location, and condition. Blockchain ensures this data remains tamper-proof and accessible to all relevant stakeholders, fostering a higher level of trust, efficiency, and responsiveness within the supply chain.

This powerful combination enhances inventory control by reducing errors, optimizing stock levels, and improving decision-making based on reliable data. The use of blockchain and IoT together provides a competitive edge, allowing businesses to achieve greater accuracy, accountability, and customer satisfaction. As more industries adopt this technology, the standards for inventory management will continue to evolve, setting a new benchmark for real-time data integrity and traceability in supply chains.

By embracing blockchain-IoT integration, companies can create resilient, agile, and transparent supply chains that are well-suited for the demands of modern commerce.

Chapter 10: Enhancing Data Security and Privacy in Inventory

- *Blockchain's Security Features: Data Encryption, Immutable Ledgers*
- *Ensuring Data Privacy and Confidentiality in Inventory Records*
- *Compliance with Data Protection Regulations*

Data security and privacy are critical concerns in modern inventory management, especially with increasing digitalization and the integration of advanced technologies. As inventory systems become more connected and data-driven, they are also more vulnerable to cyber threats, data breaches, and unauthorized access. Blockchain technology, with its inherent security features like data encryption, decentralized ledgers, and immutability, provides a robust foundation for protecting inventory data. This chapter explores blockchain's unique security features, strategies to ensure data privacy and confidentiality in inventory records, and ways to comply with data protection regulations.

Blockchain's Security Features: Data Encryption and Immutable Ledgers

One of blockchain's key strengths is its ability to provide a secure, tamper-resistant framework for managing data. This capability is essential in inventory management, where accurate and trustworthy data is critical for operational efficiency and stakeholder confidence. Blockchain employs several powerful security features, including data encryption, immutability, and consensus mechanisms, all of which contribute to a more secure inventory management system.

1. Data Encryption

Blockchain technology relies on advanced cryptographic techniques to protect data. Each transaction on a blockchain is encrypted using complex algorithms, ensuring that data cannot be easily deciphered by unauthorized parties. Data encryption enhances security in several ways:

Protects Sensitive Inventory Data: Details about inventory levels, supplier contracts, and order information are kept secure, reducing the risk of data breaches or theft.

Access Control: Only authorized users with the correct encryption keys can access specific data, which helps maintain control over who can view or modify inventory information.

For example, a warehouse system on a blockchain may encrypt all data related to stock levels and shipment records, ensuring only authorized warehouse and supply chain managers can access this information. This prevents malicious actors from intercepting data, modifying records, or exploiting sensitive information for fraudulent purposes.

2. Immutable Ledgers

Immutability is another critical security feature of blockchain technology. Once a record is created and validated on the blockchain, it cannot be altered or deleted. This immutability ensures that data is trustworthy, as each record is permanent and time-stamped.

Prevents Fraud and Tampering: Immutable records help eliminate fraudulent activity, as every transaction is securely logged and verified by the network.

Builds Trust Among Stakeholders: Since data on the blockchain cannot be retroactively changed, it fosters transparency and trust in the inventory management process. All parties can trust that the information they access is accurate and has not been tampered with.

In practice, immutable ledgers are valuable in preventing common issues in inventory management, such as "ghost stock," where records show inventory that doesn't exist. By creating an unchangeable record of every item and movement, blockchain prevents discrepancies and enhances accuracy.

3. Decentralization and Consensus Mechanisms

Blockchain's decentralized nature means that data is not stored in a central location but is distributed across multiple nodes in the network.

This decentralization, combined with consensus mechanisms, strengthens data security:

Reduces Single Points of Failure: In a decentralized system, no single server or database holds all the inventory data. This makes it more difficult for hackers to access or corrupt the system, as they would need to breach a majority of nodes simultaneously.

Enhanced Data Integrity: Consensus mechanisms, such as Proof of Work (PoW) or Proof of Stake (PoS), ensure that data is validated by multiple participants in the network. Only transactions approved by the network consensus are added to the blockchain, which prevents unauthorized changes.

For inventory systems, decentralization and consensus mechanisms ensure that data is secure, accurate, and validated by all stakeholders. This reduces the risk of inaccurate stock records or undetected changes in inventory status.

Ensuring Data Privacy and Confidentiality in Inventory Records

While blockchain offers robust security, ensuring privacy and confidentiality within inventory records is also essential. In an era of stringent data protection laws and heightened customer expectations, businesses must handle inventory data with care, especially when sensitive details about products, quantities, or supplier contracts are involved. Blockchain technology provides several mechanisms to protect data privacy and confidentiality in inventory management.

1. Permissioned Blockchains for Privacy Control

Public blockchains allow anyone to participate and view transactions, which may not be ideal for companies needing to protect inventory data. Permissioned blockchains, however, offer more control over who can access data and participate in the network.

Restricted Access: In a permissioned blockchain, only authorized participants can join the network. This restriction ensures that inventory data is shared only with verified stakeholders, such as suppliers, distributors, and internal staff.

Role-Based Permissions: Access to data can be managed at various levels, allowing different stakeholders to view only the information they need. For example, suppliers may have access to product availability data but not to the financial details of contracts.

2. Zero-Knowledge Proofs (ZKPs)

Zero-knowledge proofs are a cryptographic technique that allows one party to prove to another that they know a specific piece of information without revealing the information itself. In inventory management, ZKPs enable companies to verify inventory data with external partners without disclosing sensitive details.

For instance, a retailer could prove to a supplier that they have a sufficient quantity of items in stock without revealing the exact number. This allows for secure data sharing while maintaining confidentiality.

3. Data Masking and Encryption Techniques

Blockchain systems often incorporate data masking or encryption to further protect privacy. Data masking involves obscuring certain parts of a dataset so that only authorized users can interpret it.

Selective Disclosure: Only essential information is shared with specific parties, which is useful in scenarios where suppliers need to know stock availability without accessing the complete inventory list.

Enhanced Security for Sensitive Information: Data masking ensures that sensitive inventory information, such as stock volumes, supplier pricing, and demand forecasts, is kept confidential and only accessible to authorized individuals.

By implementing these privacy-preserving techniques, blockchain enables businesses to maintain confidentiality while still providing visibility into the supply chain for authorized users.

Compliance with Data Protection Regulations

With data privacy regulations becoming increasingly stringent worldwide, organizations must ensure their inventory management practices comply with laws like the General Data Protection Regulation (GDPR) in the EU and the California Consumer Privacy Act (CCPA) in the US. Blockchain can support compliance, though there are specific considerations to address due to the technology's unique nature.

1. GDPR and the Right to Be Forgotten

The GDPR includes a "right to be forgotten," which allows individuals to request the deletion of their personal data. Blockchain's immutability presents challenges here, as data cannot be deleted once it's recorded. Companies can address this by using strategies such as:

Off-Chain Storage: Storing sensitive personal data off-chain while keeping a hashed reference on the blockchain allows for data deletion upon request without compromising the integrity of the blockchain.

Tokenization and Encryption: Using tokens to represent data on the blockchain and encrypting them helps protect personal information.

Sensitive data remains off-chain, while only the essential information for tracking inventory transactions is retained on the blockchain.

2. Data Minimization Principles

Data minimization, which is central to regulations like GDPR, requires companies to collect only the data necessary for their purposes. Blockchain's ability to store minimal, essential information without revealing personal details aligns well with this principle. Companies can employ:

Selective Data Sharing: By leveraging role-based permissions and zero-knowledge proofs, businesses can restrict data access to only what is required.

Audit Trails for Compliance Verification: Blockchain's transparency provides an automatic audit trail, making it easier for organizations to demonstrate compliance during audits or investigations.

3. Cross-Border Data Transfers and Privacy Shield Frameworks

Blockchain's decentralized nature may involve data storage across borders, which raises concerns about data transfer regulations. Using permissioned blockchains within specific regions can help address cross-border data compliance. For instance, a company could limit access to its blockchain network based on geographic location to meet regional data privacy requirements.

Blockchain as a Tool for Compliance Transparency

In addition to meeting regulatory requirements, blockchain enhances transparency for regulators. The technology's traceability feature makes it easier to track data transactions, inventory movements, and access history. This transparency allows companies to show regulators that they are following data protection practices, ensuring accountability and trust.

Blockchain technology offers robust solutions for enhancing data security and privacy in inventory management. Its core features—such as data encryption, immutability, and decentralization—address many of the challenges faced by traditional inventory systems. At the same time, privacy-preserving techniques, like permissioned blockchains and zero-knowledge proofs, allow businesses to maintain confidentiality while sharing necessary data with trusted partners.

As regulatory landscapes continue to evolve, blockchain can be an asset for compliance, providing an immutable record that meets data protection laws. By adopting blockchain in their inventory management systems, organizations can build a secure, compliant, and transparent supply chain that meets modern security and privacy standards.

Chapter 11: Fraud Prevention and Risk Reduction with Blockchain

- ➤ Challenges of Fraud in Traditional Inventory Systems
- ➤ Blockchain for Enhanced Verification and Fraud Detection
- ➤ Reducing Risks of Counterfeit Products in the Supply Chain

Fraud poses a significant threat to inventory management, costing businesses millions in lost revenue, compromised product quality, and damaged brand reputation. Traditional inventory systems face numerous challenges in detecting and preventing fraud due to limited transparency, lack of real-time data, and inefficient verification processes. Blockchain technology offers a transformative approach to mitigating these challenges by providing enhanced verification, data security, and transparency. This chapter examines the primary challenges of fraud in conventional inventory systems, explores how blockchain can enhance fraud detection, and highlights ways blockchain can reduce the risks of counterfeit products infiltrating the supply chain.

Challenges of Fraud in Traditional Inventory Systems

In traditional inventory management, fraud can take various forms, from inventory theft and misrepresentation to the sale of counterfeit goods. These fraudulent activities can occur at multiple points along the supply chain, from suppliers and manufacturers to warehouses and retail outlets. Some of the main challenges in detecting and preventing fraud in traditional inventory systems include:

1. Lack of Transparency Across the Supply Chain

Traditional inventory systems often involve multiple intermediaries and stakeholders, making it challenging to trace products back to their origin or verify their authenticity. This lack of transparency increases the risk of fraud, as dishonest actors can manipulate records, substitute counterfeit products, or misreport inventory levels.

2. Manual and Paper-Based Processes

In many companies, inventory records are still maintained through manual or paper-based processes, which are prone to human error, manipulation, and tampering. This can lead to discrepancies in inventory data and make it difficult to trace the source of fraudulent activity.

3. Limited Real-Time Tracking and Monitoring

Traditional inventory systems lack the capability for real-time tracking, making it challenging to monitor the status and location of products as they move through the supply chain. Without real-time data, it is harder to detect suspicious activities, such as unauthorized product substitutions, delays, or diversions that may indicate fraudulent practices.

4. Complex Verification Processes

Verifying the authenticity of products and inventory data can be complex and time-consuming, especially when multiple suppliers and intermediaries are involved. Traditional systems lack a standardized, reliable way to authenticate products, which increases the risk of counterfeit goods entering the supply chain.

These challenges contribute to a higher risk of fraud, with costly consequences for businesses, including revenue losses, reputational damage, and compromised customer trust. By addressing these issues, blockchain technology can help reduce fraud and enhance the overall integrity of inventory management.

Blockchain for Enhanced Verification and Fraud Detection

Blockchain technology offers several features that make it ideal for combating fraud in inventory management. These include its decentralized structure, immutability, and transparency, which together create a robust framework for detecting and preventing fraudulent activities.

1. Decentralization and Trustless Verification

Blockchain operates on a decentralized network, meaning that no single entity has control over the entire system. This decentralization reduces the risk of fraud by ensuring that multiple participants validate transactions independently. In an inventory context, this trustless verification process makes it difficult for a single actor to manipulate data without detection.

For example, in a permissioned blockchain, multiple stakeholders (e.g., suppliers, manufacturers, and retailers) can validate inventory data without relying on a central authority. Each transaction is verified and agreed upon by the network, which helps prevent fraudulent entries or alterations.

2. Immutability and Tamper-Resistance

One of the most powerful features of blockchain is its immutability, meaning that once a transaction is recorded, it cannot be altered or deleted. This characteristic makes it nearly impossible for fraudulent actors to alter inventory records after the fact. Immutability is crucial for maintaining a reliable and transparent record of all inventory movements and transactions.

For instance, if a supplier delivers a shipment, the transaction details (such as product ID, quantity, and timestamp) are recorded on the blockchain. Any attempt to alter these details would be rejected by the network, ensuring that the original record remains intact. This transparency helps maintain data integrity and prevents unauthorized changes, which is essential for fraud detection.

3. Real-Time Data Access and Monitoring

Blockchain enables real-time access to inventory data, allowing companies to monitor products and transactions as they occur. This real-time visibility is vital for detecting suspicious activities and responding quickly to potential fraud.

For example, a retail company can track product movement from manufacturing to delivery. If a product is diverted to an unauthorized location or does not arrive as expected, the discrepancy is immediately visible on the blockchain. This level of visibility allows for faster detection of irregularities and prevents fraud from going undetected for long periods.

4. Smart Contracts for Automated Verification

Smart contracts are programmable contracts stored on the blockchain that automatically execute transactions when specific conditions are met. In inventory management, smart contracts can be used to enforce business rules, such as verifying the authenticity of a product or triggering an alert when there is an inventory discrepancy.

For instance, a smart contract could automatically verify that a supplier's shipment matches the order specifications before it is accepted into inventory. If the quantity, product specifications, or other criteria do not match, the smart contract can trigger an alert or block the transaction. This automation reduces the risk of human error and enhances fraud prevention.

Reducing Risks of Counterfeit Products in the Supply Chain

Counterfeit products are a major concern for many industries, from pharmaceuticals and electronics to luxury goods. These fake products not only damage brand reputation but also pose safety risks to consumers. Blockchain provides a reliable solution to mitigate the risks of counterfeit products by offering end-to-end traceability and authentication capabilities.

1. End-to-End Traceability for Product Authenticity

Blockchain's ability to create a permanent, transparent record of each product's journey across the supply chain helps ensure authenticity. By recording each step in the product's lifecycle, blockchain enables companies to trace a product's origin, manufacturing process, and movement across suppliers and distributors. This end-to-end traceability allows businesses and consumers alike to verify the authenticity of a product.

For example, a pharmaceutical company can use blockchain to record the manufacturing date, batch number, and transportation details of each drug. When the product reaches the end consumer, they can scan a QR code to access the blockchain record and verify its authenticity. This traceability helps protect against counterfeit products and gives consumers confidence in the product's legitimacy.

2. Digital Product Authentication

Blockchain can assign unique digital identities or "tokens" to physical products, making it easier to verify their authenticity. This process, known as tokenization, involves representing a product as a digital asset on the blockchain. Each token contains important product details, including origin, ownership, and transaction history.

In the fashion industry, for instance, luxury brands can create digital certificates for high-end products like handbags or watches. Each certificate is stored on the blockchain and can be transferred only by the brand or authorized retailers. When a consumer purchases the item, they receive a digital certificate that confirms its authenticity, making it difficult for counterfeit goods to enter the market.

3. Combating Diversion Fraud

Diversion fraud occurs when products intended for specific markets are illegally diverted to other regions, often to evade taxes or maximize profits. Blockchain helps prevent diversion fraud by providing a transparent record of each product's destination, enabling businesses to track and enforce regional distribution restrictions.

For instance, a company that exports goods to different markets can use blockchain to enforce geographical restrictions through smart contracts. If an item intended for a specific market is diverted to another, the blockchain record will reflect the discrepancy, and automated alerts can be triggered. This level of control reduces the risk of diversion fraud and ensures products are delivered to their intended destinations.

4. Reducing "Double-Spending" and Inventory Manipulation

In traditional systems, dishonest actors may manipulate inventory records to "double-spend" items—selling the same item multiple times or selling non-existent inventory. Blockchain eliminates this risk by creating a single, shared ledger that tracks each inventory item in real time. Because blockchain is a single source of truth, it is nearly impossible to create fraudulent duplicate records.

For example, if a company's inventory includes 100 units of a specific item, each unit is uniquely recorded on the blockchain. Selling or moving one of these items automatically updates the blockchain, ensuring there is no duplicate record for the same unit. This transparency makes it easy to detect discrepancies and prevents manipulation.

Blockchain technology provides a secure, transparent, and decentralized solution for combating fraud and reducing risks in inventory management. By addressing key challenges in traditional inventory systems—such as lack of transparency, limited real-time tracking, and complex verification processes—blockchain enables companies to strengthen their defenses against fraud. With features like immutable records, end-to-end traceability, and digital authentication, blockchain enhances fraud prevention, reduces counterfeit risks, and improves overall inventory security.

As businesses continue to adopt blockchain in their inventory management practices, they can expect greater accuracy, accountability, and trust throughout the supply chain. By leveraging blockchain's unique capabilities, companies can protect their assets, reduce financial losses, and ensure the integrity of their inventory systems. In doing so, they not only strengthen their competitive position but also contribute to a more transparent and trustworthy global supply chain.

Chapter 12: Blockchain in Quality Control and Compliance Management

- ➢ *Using Blockchain for Quality Assurance and Product Standards*
- ➢ *Tracking Compliance with Regulatory Standards*
- ➢ *Benefits for High-Value or Regulated Products*

In inventory management, quality control and compliance are critical factors that directly impact product reliability, customer satisfaction, and regulatory adherence. Blockchain technology has emerged as a transformative tool that can bring unprecedented levels of transparency, traceability, and accountability to quality control and compliance management. By enabling secure and immutable records, blockchain allows companies to maintain product standards, adhere to regulatory requirements, and ensure consistent quality across the supply chain. This chapter will explore how blockchain can enhance quality assurance, track compliance with regulatory standards, and provide significant benefits for high-value or regulated products.

Using Blockchain for Quality Assurance and Product Standards

Quality control is essential for any business that aims to meet customer expectations and protect its brand reputation. Traditional quality assurance systems, however, often struggle with data integrity, delayed reporting, and limited traceability across supply chains. Blockchain technology addresses these challenges by creating a transparent, tamper-proof record of every stage of the production process. This level of traceability allows companies to verify that each product meets quality standards before it reaches the consumer.

1. Immutable Quality Records

Blockchain's core feature of immutability means that once data is recorded on the ledger, it cannot be altered or deleted. This is particularly valuable for quality control because it prevents dishonest actors from manipulating data to cover up defects or inconsistencies. Immutable quality records ensure that all stakeholders have access to accurate and verifiable information, building trust in the company's quality assurance processes.

For example, in the food industry, companies can record details about each batch of raw materials, processing steps, and quality checks on the blockchain. If an issue is identified at any stage, the blockchain record provides a comprehensive history that can be reviewed to pinpoint the source of the problem. This approach not only simplifies quality audits but also prevents fraudulent practices like mislabeling or tampering with records.

2. Real-Time Quality Monitoring and Alerts

Blockchain enables real-time quality monitoring by integrating with Internet of Things (IoT) devices that capture data from the production line, warehouses, and distribution centers. Sensors connected to IoT devices can monitor environmental factors such as temperature, humidity, and handling conditions to ensure that products are consistently maintained within quality standards. The collected data is then recorded on the blockchain in real-time, allowing for continuous quality assurance.

For instance, in the pharmaceutical industry, maintaining precise temperature control is crucial for drugs and vaccines. IoT sensors placed in storage facilities can monitor temperature levels, and any deviation from acceptable limits is recorded on the blockchain. Smart contracts can automatically trigger alerts when quality standards are compromised, enabling rapid intervention to prevent compromised products from reaching consumers.

3. Standardization and Certification

Blockchain helps standardize quality control processes by providing a common platform where stakeholders can access uniform data on product standards, certifications, and inspections. This level of standardization is especially beneficial in complex supply chains that span multiple countries and regulatory environments. Certifications and inspection results can be recorded on the blockchain to verify compliance with industry standards and assure customers of product quality.

For example, a company manufacturing electronic components may be required to meet international standards such as ISO 9001 for quality management. The certification data can be stored on the blockchain, allowing customers and regulators to confirm that the company meets these standards. This transparent certification process fosters customer confidence and simplifies regulatory compliance across global supply chains.

Tracking Compliance with Regulatory Standards

Compliance with regulatory standards is a key requirement in industries such as pharmaceuticals, electronics, and food and beverages. However, traditional compliance management systems often rely on paper-based documentation and manual verification processes, which can be time-consuming and error-prone. Blockchain's ability to securely and transparently store compliance data makes it an ideal solution for managing regulatory adherence across the supply chain.

1. Enhanced Traceability for Compliance Verification

Blockchain allows for complete traceability of a product's journey from raw materials to final delivery. By recording each step of the process on the blockchain, companies can verify compliance with regulatory standards at each stage. If a regulatory authority requests proof of compliance, companies can quickly provide an immutable record that details each step taken to meet the required standards.

For instance, the food industry faces stringent regulations on food safety, including standards for handling, storage, and transportation. Blockchain enables companies to track every step of the production and distribution process, recording compliance checks, quality tests, and environmental conditions. This level of traceability makes it easier for companies to provide documentation that proves compliance, minimizing the risk of fines or product recalls due to non-compliance.

2. Simplifying Audits and Reporting

Blockchain streamlines the audit process by providing a single, unified record of all compliance-related activities. Auditors can access the blockchain ledger to review compliance data without needing to go through extensive paperwork or reconcile data from different systems. This saves time, reduces administrative costs, and increases the accuracy of compliance reporting.

For example, pharmaceutical companies are often required to conduct detailed audits of their supply chain to ensure compliance with regulations on drug safety and manufacturing. With blockchain, these companies can provide auditors with direct access to compliance records, including certifications, quality tests, and shipment details. This automated reporting process simplifies audits and ensures that all compliance data is easily accessible and verifiable.

3. Automating Compliance with Smart Contracts

Smart contracts, which are self-executing contracts with the terms of the agreement directly written into code, can be programmed to enforce regulatory requirements automatically. When integrated with IoT devices, smart contracts can trigger actions based on real-time data to ensure ongoing compliance with regulatory standards. This automation reduces the risk of human error and ensures that compliance is consistently maintained.

In the case of perishable goods, for example, a smart contract can be set to monitor the temperature during transport and ensure it remains within regulatory limits. If the temperature exceeds the permissible range, the smart contract could automatically trigger a compliance alert or even halt further shipment to prevent non-compliant goods from reaching the market. This level of automation ensures that companies adhere to regulatory requirements without relying on manual oversight.

Benefits for High-Value or Regulated Products

Certain products, particularly those in high-value or highly regulated industries, require stringent quality control and compliance measures due to their potential risks and economic impact. Blockchain technology provides additional benefits for managing these products, offering an efficient way to track quality, verify authenticity, and comply with regulatory requirements.

1. Protecting High-Value Assets

For high-value assets like luxury goods, electronics, and rare materials, authenticity is a critical concern. Blockchain's transparent and immutable records allow companies to create a digital history for each product, preventing fraud, theft, and counterfeiting. With unique digital identities, companies can track every stage of a product's lifecycle, from manufacturing to sale, offering customers assurance of authenticity and quality.

For instance, luxury fashion brands can use blockchain to authenticate high-end items, such as designer bags or jewelry. By assigning each product a digital certificate on the blockchain, these brands enable customers to verify the item's origin and manufacturing details, protecting against counterfeit goods.

2. Ensuring Safety for Regulated Products

Industries such as pharmaceuticals and medical devices are highly regulated due to the potential risks associated with compromised product quality. Blockchain's traceability features allow for strict monitoring and documentation of every step in the production process, ensuring compliance with safety and quality regulations.

In the pharmaceutical industry, for example, blockchain can be used to document every stage of a drug's production and distribution, from raw materials to the finished product. This end-to-end traceability ensures that drugs meet regulatory standards and provides an unalterable record for audits and recalls. If a batch is found to be defective, companies can use blockchain to trace the issue back to its source, facilitating targeted recalls and reducing harm to patients.

3. Streamlining Compliance in High-Risk Industries

In industries where regulatory compliance is critical and non-compliance can result in severe consequences, blockchain can provide an efficient way to streamline compliance management. By automating compliance verification and maintaining accurate records, blockchain reduces the risk of fines, penalties, and reputational damage.

For example, in the aviation industry, companies must comply with strict safety standards for parts and equipment. Blockchain can track each part's manufacturing details, quality inspections, and maintenance history, creating a comprehensive record that verifies compliance with safety regulations. This transparency helps companies avoid the use of faulty parts, reducing the risk of accidents and improving overall safety.

Blockchain technology offers a transformative solution for enhancing quality control and compliance management in inventory systems. By providing immutable, transparent records and enabling real-time monitoring, blockchain addresses key challenges in traditional quality assurance and compliance processes. Through features like smart contracts and end-to-end traceability, blockchain helps companies maintain product quality, adhere to regulatory standards, and reduce the risk of non-compliance, particularly in high-value or regulated industries.

As companies continue to adopt blockchain technology for quality and compliance management, they stand to gain significant benefits in terms of operational efficiency, cost savings, and customer trust. By leveraging blockchain's unique capabilities, businesses can create more reliable, transparent, and secure inventory systems that meet the demands of modern supply chains. This approach not only enhances product quality and compliance but also strengthens the resilience and integrity of the entire supply chain network.

Chapter 13: Blockchain for Supplier Collaboration and Transparency

- How Blockchain Enhances Collaboration Across Stakeholders
- Improving Supplier Accountability and Trust
- Role of Blockchain in Streamlining Supplier Relationships

In today's globalized economy, supply chains are composed of numerous stakeholders, from suppliers and manufacturers to distributors and retailers. Efficient collaboration and transparency among these parties are essential to maintain smooth operations and high standards in inventory management. Blockchain technology provides a powerful framework for enhancing supplier collaboration, improving accountability, and fostering trust. By offering a shared, secure, and immutable record-keeping system, blockchain facilitates clear communication and reliable data sharing among stakeholders, strengthening relationships across the supply chain. This chapter delves into how blockchain enhances collaboration, builds accountability and trust with suppliers, and streamlines supplier relationships for better inventory management.

How Blockchain Enhances Collaboration Across Stakeholders

In traditional supply chains, data is often fragmented, held in silos, and manually shared between stakeholders. This disjointed approach creates information asymmetries and delays, hindering effective collaboration. Blockchain technology enables a shift towards a more integrated and transparent system where data is shared in real-time across all authorized participants. With a decentralized network, blockchain allows all stakeholders to access a single source of truth regarding inventory levels, shipments, production schedules, and quality control.

1. A Unified Platform for Data Sharing

Blockchain's distributed ledger serves as a unified platform for stakeholders to access and share real-time data. This shared platform eliminates the need for intermediaries, reduces information asymmetries, and ensures that all participants are working with the same, up-to-date information. For example, if a supplier logs a shipment of raw materials onto the blockchain, manufacturers and logistics providers can instantly access this information, facilitating faster coordination.

For instance, in the automotive industry, where suppliers provide parts from different regions, blockchain can record the real-time location and status of shipments, allowing manufacturers to prepare for production or make necessary adjustments in case of delays. This integrated information flow helps suppliers and manufacturers work in sync, reducing disruptions and improving overall efficiency.

2. Improved Decision-Making through Transparency

Transparency in data fosters trust and enables better decision-making among supply chain participants. Blockchain allows each stakeholder to view the inventory and transaction records of others, which helps companies make informed choices about inventory management, supplier selection, and risk assessment. Transparent access to this data also reduces misunderstandings and helps stakeholders collaborate more effectively to resolve issues when they arise.

In the food industry, for example, transparency regarding the source and handling of ingredients is crucial. Blockchain can provide a detailed view of the supply chain from farm to table, allowing food manufacturers, retailers, and consumers to verify the origin and quality of food products. By fostering a culture of openness, blockchain helps build stronger, more collaborative relationships between suppliers and manufacturers, ultimately enhancing the quality and safety of products.

3. Streamlined Communication through Smart Contracts

Smart contracts, which execute automatically when predefined conditions are met, simplify and automate communication between stakeholders. By encoding rules, payment terms, and delivery deadlines into smart contracts, companies can reduce the risk of delays, errors, and disputes. When a supplier fulfills an order, the blockchain-based contract can automatically release payments or trigger the next steps in the supply chain, ensuring smooth and timely operations.

For instance, in the electronics industry, where parts are often sourced from multiple suppliers, smart contracts can be used to automatically approve quality checks, release payments, or reorder components when inventory drops below a certain level. This automation not only streamlines communication but also reduces the administrative burden on both parties, allowing them to focus on their core activities.

Improving Supplier Accountability and Trust

Trust between suppliers and buyers is crucial for a reliable supply chain. However, traditional supply chain models often lack accountability due to fragmented information and inconsistent data sharing. Blockchain's immutable ledger and transparency features increase accountability by creating a permanent record of all transactions and activities. This level of traceability helps companies hold suppliers accountable for quality, timely delivery, and ethical practices.

1. Immutable Record of Supplier Transactions

Blockchain's immutability ensures that records of transactions and interactions with suppliers cannot be altered or deleted. This feature is particularly valuable in cases where accountability is essential, such as tracking the quality of raw materials, adherence to delivery schedules, or compliance with regulatory standards. By creating an unalterable history of transactions, blockchain helps companies verify that suppliers are meeting their obligations.

For example, in the pharmaceutical industry, ensuring that suppliers adhere to strict quality standards is critical. A blockchain record can verify that each batch of raw materials has passed the necessary quality checks before it is used in production. If any discrepancies arise, the company can trace the issue back to its source and hold the supplier accountable, ensuring better compliance with quality standards.

2. Enhanced Verification for Ethical and Sustainable Practices

Many companies are committed to ethical sourcing and sustainability, but verifying these practices across a complex supply chain can be challenging. Blockchain provides a transparent record of each supplier's activities, allowing companies to verify ethical sourcing practices and ensure suppliers meet sustainability standards. This verification builds trust in the supply chain and demonstrates a commitment to responsible business practices.

For example, fashion brands that prioritize sustainable sourcing can use blockchain to track the journey of raw materials, such as cotton or leather, from the source to the finished product. This tracking enables brands to ensure that their suppliers are adhering to ethical practices, such as fair labor standards and eco-friendly production methods. By improving accountability, blockchain enhances supplier relationships and strengthens the brand's reputation.

3. Facilitating Trust through Transparency

Blockchain's transparency fosters trust between suppliers and buyers by providing real-time, verifiable data about each transaction and shipment. This transparency eliminates the "black box" effect, where stakeholders lack visibility into key parts of the supply chain, leading to misunderstandings and mistrust. By providing open access to data, blockchain helps suppliers and buyers develop a trusting relationship that is crucial for long-term collaboration.

In the electronics industry, where parts are often sourced globally, transparency is crucial to maintaining trust. Blockchain can document the origin, specifications, and handling of each component, giving buyers confidence that they are receiving genuine, high-quality parts. This transparency mitigates the risk of counterfeit components, fostering trust and reinforcing accountability in supplier relationships.

Role of Blockchain in Streamlining Supplier Relationships

Supplier relationships are the backbone of efficient inventory management. Traditional supplier relationship management is often hindered by delays, miscommunications, and complex administrative processes. Blockchain technology helps streamline these relationships by automating workflows, enhancing data access, and reducing the reliance on intermediaries.

1. Reducing Administrative Overhead with Smart Contracts

Smart contracts eliminate much of the administrative work associated with supplier relationships. By automating processes like order verification, payment releases, and contract renewals, blockchain reduces the need for constant manual intervention. This automation allows companies to maintain efficient relationships with suppliers, free from the delays and errors associated with traditional administrative processes.

For instance, a manufacturing company could use blockchain to manage its suppliers' orders through automated smart contracts. When a supplier ships an order and the goods meet quality standards, the blockchain can automatically initiate payment according to the terms of the contract. This process reduces the time and resources spent on managing invoices, payments, and contract renewals, creating a more streamlined relationship with suppliers.

2. Enhancing Supplier Performance Management

Blockchain's transparent records allow companies to monitor supplier performance over time. By tracking metrics like delivery accuracy, quality standards, and lead times, companies can identify high-performing suppliers and address issues with underperforming ones. This level of visibility enables companies to make informed decisions about supplier selection and retention, leading to stronger partnerships and more efficient inventory management.

For example, in the automotive industry, manufacturers often depend on just-in-time deliveries from suppliers to keep production lines running smoothly. Blockchain can track delivery times and quality checks for each shipment, providing a clear record of supplier performance. This data helps manufacturers hold suppliers to high standards and rewards those that consistently meet expectations, fostering a collaborative and performance-oriented relationship.

3. Building Collaborative Supplier Networks

Blockchain fosters a collaborative environment by enabling secure, transparent, and real-time data sharing across the supply chain. This collaboration allows suppliers and buyers to work more closely, aligning their goals and sharing insights that improve inventory management. By creating a network of trusted suppliers who share common standards and expectations, companies can build resilient supply chains that respond more effectively to market demands.

For instance, a retail company can use blockchain to create a collaborative network of suppliers who share inventory data and demand forecasts. This data-sharing enables suppliers to anticipate demand fluctuations and adjust their production schedules accordingly, reducing stockouts and overproduction. By fostering a collaborative network, blockchain strengthens supplier relationships and enhances inventory efficiency across the supply chain.

Blockchain technology offers a comprehensive solution for enhancing supplier collaboration, improving accountability, and streamlining relationships in inventory management. Through features like real-time data sharing, immutable records, and smart contracts, blockchain enables stakeholders to work more efficiently and transparently, fostering trust and cooperation. By improving supplier accountability, blockchain not only strengthens supplier relationships but also enhances the overall integrity and resilience of the supply chain.

As companies continue to adopt blockchain for supplier collaboration, they can expect to see improvements in efficiency, reduced administrative burdens, and stronger, more reliable supplier networks. Ultimately, blockchain's impact on supplier relationships goes beyond data management; it fosters a culture of transparency, trust, and collaboration that is essential for navigating the complexities of modern inventory management.

Chapter 14: Reducing Operational Costs with Blockchain

- ➢ *Cost-saving Opportunities from Automated Processes*
- ➢ *Reducing Inventory Shrinkage and Stockouts*
- ➢ *Efficiency Gains in Inventory Replenishment and Stock Optimization*

In the highly competitive and cost-sensitive world of supply chain management, reducing operational costs is a critical objective for companies seeking to remain profitable and efficient. Inventory management represents one of the most significant cost centers in the supply chain, affecting both upstream and downstream processes. Traditional inventory systems often struggle with inefficiencies that lead to increased labor costs, stockouts, overstocking, and inventory shrinkage, all of which reduce profitability. Blockchain technology offers a promising solution to these issues by automating processes, providing real-time visibility, and enhancing data security. Through blockchain, companies can achieve significant cost savings by streamlining operations, reducing shrinkage, and optimizing inventory management.

This chapter explores how blockchain technology helps companies reduce operational costs through three main avenues: automated processes, minimizing inventory shrinkage and stockouts, and achieving efficiency gains in inventory replenishment and stock optimization.

Cost-saving Opportunities from Automated Processes

One of the most transformative aspects of blockchain in inventory management is its ability to automate processes traditionally handled through manual intervention. These automations are facilitated by smart contracts — self-executing contracts coded onto the blockchain that automatically execute actions once certain predefined conditions are met. Automating these workflows can reduce human errors, minimize labor costs, and accelerate processes that otherwise consume significant time and resources.

1. Automating Order Processing and Fulfillment

Order processing and fulfillment are typically complex and time-intensive processes involving several steps, including order validation, billing, payment processing, and inventory allocation. In a traditional inventory management system, these steps often require manual verification and approvals, which add to labor costs and increase the risk of delays. With blockchain and smart contracts, these tasks can be automated, reducing the time and cost involved.

For example, when an order is placed, a smart contract on the blockchain can automatically verify inventory levels, allocate the necessary stock, generate an invoice, and trigger the billing and payment process. Once the payment is confirmed, the system can notify the warehouse for dispatch. This automation reduces the dependency on manual labor for routine tasks, speeds up order processing, and enables more consistent service levels without requiring additional resources.

2. Enhancing Supplier Payments and Invoicing

The payment and invoicing processes between suppliers and buyers are often plagued by delays, errors, and the need for multiple reconciliations. Traditional invoicing typically relies on multiple touchpoints, with invoices passing through several departments for approval before final payment is released. Blockchain can streamline this process by embedding payment terms into smart contracts. For instance, when a supplier delivers goods and the items are verified, the blockchain can automatically release payments based on the agreed terms.

This approach reduces delays, eliminates errors, and minimizes the administrative cost associated with invoice processing. Furthermore, automated payments strengthen relationships with suppliers by ensuring timely payments, reducing disputes, and establishing clear accountability. Over time, the cost savings from reducing labor costs associated with processing payments and minimizing disputes can be substantial.

3. Reducing Administrative Overhead with Automated Compliance Checks

Inventory management in regulated industries, such as pharmaceuticals and food, involves stringent compliance requirements. Adhering to these regulations often demands significant administrative resources to ensure proper documentation, labeling, and storage. Blockchain's immutable ledger and real-time data tracking streamline compliance by providing an automated and auditable trail for each transaction, eliminating the need for extensive manual documentation checks. Blockchain also enables real-time monitoring of regulatory compliance, such as temperature conditions in food storage, through integration with IoT sensors. Automated compliance checks reduce administrative overhead and prevent costly compliance violations.

Reducing Inventory Shrinkage and Stockouts

Inventory shrinkage, caused by theft, fraud, damaged goods, and administrative errors, is a major contributor to operational costs in inventory management. Similarly, stockouts, which occur when items are not available to meet demand, lead to lost sales and a negative impact on customer satisfaction. Blockchain's transparency, traceability, and security features can play a crucial role in addressing these issues, helping companies reduce both shrinkage and stockouts.

1. Enhanced Security and Fraud Prevention

Blockchain's decentralized and immutable nature makes it highly secure, which is essential for preventing fraud and theft in the supply chain. In a traditional inventory system, data can be easily tampered with, making it difficult to verify inventory records accurately. Blockchain's ledger is immutable, meaning that once data is added, it cannot be altered or deleted. This transparency reduces the opportunity for fraud and unauthorized activities.

For instance, blockchain can track each step in the supply chain, from raw material sourcing to final delivery. This granular tracking makes it more challenging for bad actors to manipulate inventory records or misreport stock levels. By reducing fraud and theft, companies can cut down on inventory shrinkage, resulting in cost savings and improved financial performance.

2. Real-time Inventory Monitoring to Reduce Stockouts

Stockouts occur when inventory levels fall below demand, leading to lost sales and customer dissatisfaction. In traditional systems, stockouts often result from delayed or inaccurate data, which prevents timely reordering. Blockchain addresses this issue by providing real-time, transparent data on inventory levels accessible to all stakeholders. This visibility ensures that inventory data is always up-to-date, enabling companies to react quickly to fluctuations in demand and avoid stockouts.

For example, in the retail industry, blockchain can provide real-time inventory visibility across multiple stores, allowing managers to see where stock is low and needs replenishment. Real-time visibility allows companies to avoid lost sales by keeping popular items in stock, thereby boosting revenue and reducing the costs associated with emergency restocking or expedited shipping.

3. Improved Inventory Accuracy

Inaccurate inventory records are a common challenge in traditional systems, often leading to overstocking or stockouts. Manual errors, delays in updating records, and discrepancies between different systems contribute to inaccuracies, increasing carrying costs and operational inefficiencies. Blockchain's real-time, synchronized ledger ensures that inventory records are accurate and up-to-date across all locations and stakeholders.

For example, in a warehouse setting, every product movement — from receiving goods to dispatching them for delivery — can be recorded on the blockchain, creating an accurate, real-time record of stock levels. This improved accuracy enables companies to make more informed decisions about purchasing and stocking, reducing costs associated with excess inventory and mitigating the risk of stockouts.

Efficiency Gains in Inventory Replenishment and Stock Optimization

Optimizing inventory levels is essential to minimize carrying costs, which include storage, insurance, and depreciation costs. Blockchain enables greater efficiency in inventory replenishment and stock optimization by providing a seamless flow of accurate, real-time information, allowing for better demand forecasting, reduced lead times, and more efficient stock allocation.

1. Demand Forecasting and Stock Replenishment

Accurate demand forecasting is crucial for effective inventory management, allowing companies to stock the right products in the right quantities. Blockchain's transparency enables companies to collect and analyze data from various stages of the supply chain, providing a comprehensive view of demand patterns, supplier performance, and inventory turnover rates. This data can be used to enhance forecasting models, ensuring that stock levels are optimized to meet anticipated demand.

For instance, a retail company could use blockchain data to analyze historical sales patterns, seasonal demand shifts, and supplier delivery times to improve demand forecasting. Enhanced forecasting reduces the likelihood of overstocking or understocking, helping companies cut down on carrying costs and avoid the need for markdowns on excess inventory.

2. Reducing Lead Times with Supplier Integration

Lead times — the period between placing an order and receiving it — play a significant role in inventory costs. Long or unpredictable lead times require companies to hold more safety stock, increasing carrying costs. Blockchain enables closer integration with suppliers by providing them with real-time data on stock levels and demand, allowing them to respond more quickly and effectively to orders.

For example, with blockchain, a supplier could receive immediate notifications when a company's stock reaches a predefined threshold, allowing for prompt order fulfillment. This close coordination reduces lead times, allowing companies to hold less safety stock and lower their carrying costs. As lead times become more predictable, companies can optimize reorder points, improving overall inventory efficiency and reducing costs.

3. Optimized Stock Allocation

Efficient stock allocation ensures that inventory is distributed to the locations where it is needed most, reducing the costs associated with overstocking or stockouts at specific sites. Blockchain's transparency enables companies to monitor inventory levels across multiple locations in real-time, ensuring that stock is allocated efficiently based on demand and sales trends.

For instance, in a multi-warehouse network, blockchain can track the exact inventory levels and demand at each location, allowing for dynamic stock allocation. A central warehouse can use this information to redistribute stock among regional warehouses based on real-time demand fluctuations. This approach reduces the need for expensive emergency shipments and ensures that each location is appropriately stocked, leading to cost savings and improved service levels.

4. Cost-effective Supplier Management and Negotiation

Blockchain's transparency into supplier performance data enables companies to negotiate better terms with suppliers. By providing data on supplier lead times, order accuracy, and quality, blockchain empowers companies to select the most reliable suppliers, negotiate cost-effective contracts, and reduce variability in the supply chain.

or instance, companies can identify suppliers with consistently reliable delivery and quality performance, which minimizes the risk of disruptions. This reliability allows companies to negotiate favorable terms, such as volume discounts or extended payment terms, that reduce procurement costs and contribute to overall cost savings.

Blockchain technology presents significant opportunities for cost savings in inventory management by automating processes, reducing shrinkage, preventing stockouts, and optimizing inventory allocation. The transparency and real-time data-sharing capabilities of blockchain allow companies to reduce their dependency on manual labor, minimize errors, and streamline communication with suppliers. By mitigating inventory shrinkage and improving forecasting accuracy, companies can reduce both stockouts and overstocking, resulting in substantial cost savings.

As companies continue to explore and implement blockchain solutions in inventory management, they stand to benefit from reduced operational costs and increased efficiency. Blockchain transforms inventory management from a cost center into a more agile, transparent, and cost-effective process, enabling businesses to stay competitive and responsive in an increasingly dynamic marketplace.

Chapter 15: Case Studies: Blockchain in Inventory Management

- *Success Stories from Various Industries (Retail, Pharma, Food, Manufacturing)*
- *Lessons Learned from Implementing Blockchain*
- *How Early Adopters Overcame Challenges*

Blockchain technology has proven to be a transformative force in inventory management, enhancing visibility, traceability, security, and efficiency across the supply chain. This chapter presents case studies from diverse industries, including retail, pharmaceuticals, food, and manufacturing, showcasing how early adopters have successfully implemented blockchain technology to overcome traditional inventory challenges. By analyzing these real-world applications, we can draw valuable lessons on how to best leverage blockchain in inventory management, the challenges companies faced, and how they addressed these obstacles.

Success Stories from Various Industries

1. Retail: Walmart's Blockchain Solution for Food Traceability

Walmart, one of the largest retail chains globally, implemented a blockchain-based traceability system to improve food safety and reduce the time needed to track contaminated products. Walmart's blockchain system, developed in collaboration with IBM, uses Hyperledger Fabric to provide end-to-end visibility and traceability for food items throughout the supply chain.

Before implementing blockchain, it would take Walmart up to seven days to trace a product's origin back through the supply chain. With blockchain, the time required to trace a food product's journey has been reduced to just a few seconds. This improvement significantly enhances Walmart's ability to quickly identify and remove potentially contaminated products from store shelves, reducing health risks to consumers.

Key Lessons Learned:

Improved Consumer Safety: Blockchain enables rapid tracing of food products, helping to quickly remove contaminated goods from circulation and prevent foodborne illness.

Streamlined Compliance: The system also simplifies compliance with regulatory requirements by providing a transparent and immutable record of the product journey, which can be shared with regulatory authorities when needed.

Collaboration with Suppliers: Walmart's success was due to its ability to bring together various suppliers onto a single platform, showcasing the importance of stakeholder collaboration in blockchain implementation.

2. Pharmaceuticals: MediLedger's Solution for Drug Traceability

The pharmaceutical industry faces significant challenges in tracking drugs through the supply chain to prevent counterfeit products from entering the market. MediLedger, a blockchain-based consortium in the pharmaceutical industry, developed a blockchain network to improve transparency and traceability for prescription drugs.

Through MediLedger, pharmaceutical companies and distributors can authenticate products at each step of the supply chain, reducing the risk of counterfeit drugs reaching consumers. This transparency is especially critical given the stringent regulatory requirements of the pharmaceutical industry. By utilizing blockchain's decentralized ledger, MediLedger enables real-time tracking of drug movement and ensures that only verified participants have access to the blockchain.

Key Lessons Learned:

Combatting Counterfeiting: Blockchain's immutability and transparency make it an effective tool for preventing counterfeit drugs, protecting both patients and brand integrity.

Regulatory Compliance: Blockchain assists companies in adhering to strict regulatory standards for drug traceability, including the U.S. Drug

Supply Chain Security Act (DSCSA), which mandates the tracking of drugs from manufacturer to pharmacy.

Industry Collaboration: MediLedger's success highlights the importance of industry-wide collaboration, as it requires multiple players — manufacturers, distributors, and pharmacies — to participate and share information securely.

3. Food: Bumble Bee Foods and Transparency in Seafood Sourcing

Bumble Bee Foods, a seafood company, implemented blockchain to improve transparency in the sourcing of tuna and other seafood products. Partnering with SAP, Bumble Bee uses blockchain to enable consumers to track the journey of their tuna from the ocean to their plate. By scanning a QR code on the product packaging, consumers can access detailed information about where the tuna was caught, who caught it, and the journey it took to reach the store.

Blockchain allows Bumble Bee Foods to verify sustainable fishing practices and ensure compliance with industry standards, offering greater transparency and building consumer trust. This traceability system also assists the company in meeting regulatory requirements for sustainable and ethical sourcing.

Key Lessons Learned:

Consumer Trust and Brand Value: Blockchain helps to increase consumer confidence by providing transparent information about product origins and sustainable practices.

Sustainability Assurance: Blockchain supports responsible sourcing, allowing companies to validate their sustainability claims and meet consumer demand for ethically sourced products.

Value-added Transparency: The implementation demonstrates that blockchain can be a powerful tool for differentiating brands by providing an added layer of transparency to consumers.

4. Manufacturing: Ford's Blockchain Pilot for Ethical Sourcing of Cobalt

Ford partnered with IBM and several other companies to launch a blockchain pilot focused on ethically sourcing cobalt, a key component in lithium-ion batteries used in electric vehicles. The blockchain system ensures that the cobalt used in Ford's batteries is sourced responsibly, without child labor or exploitative practices.

Ford's pilot program tracks the journey of cobalt from mines in the Democratic Republic of Congo through the supply chain to the end manufacturer. By providing real-time data on sourcing practices, blockchain enables Ford to demonstrate its commitment to ethical sourcing and meet growing consumer and regulatory expectations for responsible sourcing.

Key Lessons Learned:

Ethical Supply Chain Management: Blockchain can verify that materials used in manufacturing are sourced ethically, helping companies meet corporate social responsibility goals.

Compliance with Social Standards: Blockchain's transparent ledger allows companies to demonstrate compliance with social and ethical sourcing standards.

Increased Accountability: Ford's experience shows how blockchain can increase accountability among suppliers, ensuring that ethical practices are followed at each stage of the supply chain.

Lessons Learned from Implementing Blockchain

The case studies highlight several lessons that other companies can learn from early adopters:

Collaboration is Key: Many blockchain implementations require the collaboration of multiple stakeholders, from suppliers to logistics providers and regulators. Success is more likely when all parties are aligned and committed to data sharing and transparency.

Data Standardization: Blockchain requires standardized data formats and processes to be effective. Companies should work with partners to ensure consistent data practices to maximize blockchain's benefits.

Balancing Privacy and Transparency: While blockchain provides transparency, companies must also manage data privacy concerns, especially in highly regulated industries. Careful design of permissions and access controls is essential for protecting sensitive information.

Scalability and Cost: Blockchain implementations, especially in pilot stages, can be resource-intensive. Companies must carefully evaluate the scalability of blockchain solutions to ensure they are cost-effective in the long term.

Change Management and Training: Adopting blockchain requires a shift in mindset for many employees, especially those accustomed to traditional inventory practices. Providing adequate training and managing the change process can improve user acceptance and the successful adoption of blockchain technology.

How Early Adopters Overcame Challenges

1. Addressing Interoperability Issues

Interoperability — the ability of different systems to work together — is a common challenge in blockchain implementation. In the case of MediLedger, the consortium addressed this issue by adopting standards and protocols that enable seamless communication between different platforms. This standardization allows various stakeholders in the pharmaceutical supply chain to connect, share data, and validate transactions, despite using different internal systems.

2. Ensuring Data Privacy and Security

Privacy concerns are prevalent, particularly in industries like pharmaceuticals and retail, where sensitive information is shared across the supply chain. Early adopters have tackled this challenge by using permissioned blockchains, which restrict access to authorized users only. For example, MediLedger uses a permissioned blockchain that ensures only verified participants have access to the data, balancing transparency with privacy.

3. Integrating Blockchain with Existing Systems

Integrating blockchain with legacy inventory management systems can be complex. Walmart, for instance, worked with IBM to create a system that integrates blockchain data with their existing food safety protocols. This hybrid approach allowed Walmart to leverage blockchain's traceability without needing a complete overhaul of their existing infrastructure, saving time and resources.

4. Managing Regulatory Compliance

Many early adopters face the challenge of aligning blockchain implementations with regulatory requirements. The pharmaceutical industry, for example, operates under strict regulations like the DSCSA.

To ensure compliance, MediLedger worked closely with regulatory bodies, aligning its blockchain protocols with regulatory standards and ensuring that data recorded on the blockchain could be accessed by auditors and compliance officers.

5. Overcoming Initial Resistance

Blockchain represents a major shift in how inventory management data is shared and stored, and some organizations have faced internal resistance to change. Early adopters have addressed this by demonstrating blockchain's value through pilot programs that yield measurable results, such as cost savings, reduced fraud, or improved compliance. Walmart's pilot program, for example, demonstrated clear time savings in traceability, helping to secure buy-in from stakeholders across the organization.

The implementation of blockchain in inventory management is still in its early stages, but these case studies illustrate the significant advantages and challenges associated with the technology. Early adopters across industries have demonstrated blockchain's potential to enhance traceability, improve compliance, combat counterfeiting, and foster transparency. Lessons learned from these case studies show that successful blockchain adoption requires collaboration, data standardization, privacy considerations, and adaptability to overcome integration and regulatory challenges.

As more companies explore blockchain for inventory management, they can build on the experiences of these pioneers to streamline their supply chains, reduce costs, and strengthen consumer trust. With continued advancements in blockchain and an increasing emphasis on transparency and accountability in supply chains, the adoption of blockchain in inventory management is likely to grow, bringing transformative benefits across various industries.

Chapter 16: Blockchain's Role in Reverse Logistics and Returns

- *Using Blockchain for Efficient Returns Management*
- *Ensuring Transparency in Product Returns and Refunds*
- *Benefits of Blockchain in Recycling and Waste Management*

Reverse logistics, encompassing product returns, recycling, and disposal processes, plays a crucial role in the modern supply chain. Efficiently managing returns and waste is challenging, especially with traditional inventory and logistics systems that lack transparency and real-time visibility. Blockchain technology has the potential to streamline these processes, offering unique advantages for reverse logistics, including secure tracking, transparency, and efficiency in managing returns and refunds. This chapter explores how blockchain can transform reverse logistics by making returns management more efficient, ensuring transparency in product returns, and enhancing recycling and waste management efforts.

Using Blockchain for Efficient Returns Management

Efficient returns management is a key aspect of reverse logistics, as companies often face high costs and logistical complexities associated with handling product returns. Traditional returns management systems frequently rely on fragmented processes, manual data entry, and multiple intermediaries, all of which can result in delays, errors, and increased costs. Blockchain technology offers a streamlined alternative by creating a single, decentralized ledger where every participant can access accurate, real-time information on returned goods.

Streamlined Process Flow

By using blockchain, companies can simplify the returns process. For instance, when a customer initiates a return, the information is recorded on the blockchain and shared with all relevant parties, including retailers, warehouses, logistics providers, and manufacturers. This eliminates the need for back-and-forth communication and ensures that all parties are working with the same data.

Each step in the returns process—from receiving the item at a collection center to inspecting it, repackaging, and restocking or recycling—is recorded on the blockchain. This transparency helps eliminate redundant paperwork and improves efficiency by providing all stakeholders with real-time information about the return status and next steps.

Enhanced Verification and Tracking

Blockchain allows companies to authenticate returns with more accuracy. Using product-specific information, such as serial numbers, RFID tags, or QR codes, companies can record unique identifiers for each product on the blockchain. This ensures that the item being returned is legitimate and matches the original sale, reducing the risk of fraud, which is a common issue in returns management.

For example, in the electronics industry, where returned items are often high-value and prone to fraudulent returns, blockchain can verify the product's origin, warranty status, and authenticity, ensuring that the return meets the company's criteria before processing it.

Automated Smart Contracts

Blockchain can utilize smart contracts to automate key aspects of the returns process. Smart contracts are self-executing contracts with the terms of the agreement written directly into the code. When certain conditions are met, the smart contract triggers an action. For example, if a product is returned within the warranty period and meets specified conditions, a smart contract can automatically approve the refund and initiate payment processing. This automation reduces the need for manual approvals, speeds up the refund process, and enhances customer satisfaction by delivering a faster, more reliable returns experience.

Additionally, smart contracts can trigger restocking or recycling processes once the returned item is verified. This helps reduce turnaround time and ensures that products are re-entered into inventory or sent to appropriate recycling channels promptly, contributing to better inventory management.

Example in Action:

Amazon has explored using blockchain for managing returns more efficiently. By leveraging blockchain's transparency and automation, Amazon can streamline return authorizations, manage inspection processes, and facilitate quicker refunds to enhance the customer experience.

Ensuring Transparency in Product Returns and Refunds

Blockchain's decentralized and immutable nature makes it an ideal solution for enhancing transparency in product returns and refund processes. Each transaction is securely recorded on a ledger accessible to all relevant stakeholders, allowing for complete visibility into the lifecycle of a returned product.

Immutable Records for Each Return

When a customer initiates a return, blockchain can create an immutable record that includes critical information such as the date of return, reason for the return, item condition, and refund status. Since these records cannot be altered, they serve as a reliable and permanent history of each product return. This transparency is particularly valuable for companies that need to prove compliance with return policies or resolve disputes.

Real-Time Access for Customers

Blockchain technology can also benefit customers by providing them with real-time updates on the status of their return and refund. Using a blockchain-based system, customers can track their return as it moves through each stage—from drop-off to inspection, refund processing, and final resolution. This increased visibility helps build customer trust and satisfaction, as customers know exactly when to expect their refund or replacement.

Reducing Disputes and Increasing Trust

The transparency afforded by blockchain minimizes disputes related to returns and refunds. In many cases, customers may be uncertain about the status of their return or frustrated with delays, leading to disputes and complaints. By providing real-time visibility, blockchain reduces the likelihood of misunderstandings and builds trust between the company and its customers.

Additionally, blockchain enables companies to offer transparent and fair return policies. By implementing a standardized and traceable return process, companies can ensure that all customers receive equal treatment and that all returns are processed accurately and fairly.

Example in Action:

H&M, the fashion retail giant, has tested blockchain for returns management, aiming to ensure transparency for customers who wish to return products. The blockchain ledger records each step of the returns process, allowing customers to follow their items and understand how long each stage takes.

Benefits of Blockchain in Recycling and Waste Management

Reverse logistics extends beyond product returns and refunds to include recycling and waste management. Blockchain can enhance recycling programs by creating transparent records of materials and products, helping companies meet sustainability goals and comply with environmental regulations.

Tracking Recyclable Materials

Blockchain enables companies to track products that are eligible for recycling throughout their lifecycle. For example, manufacturers can use blockchain to record the type of materials used in a product, the recycling methods available, and whether the product has undergone recycling processes. This information can be shared with recyclers and disposal partners, allowing them to follow specific guidelines and ensure that products are recycled properly.

Blockchain also enables companies to track the provenance of raw materials. In industries such as electronics, where certain metals and components can be recycled and reused, blockchain can verify the origins of materials and ensure they come from recycled or ethically sourced supplies.

Supporting Circular Economy Initiatives

Blockchain can facilitate circular economy practices by creating a seamless flow of information about recycled products, reused components, and repurposed materials. In a circular economy model, companies design products to be reused or recycled at the end of their lifecycle. Blockchain can track products as they are returned, disassembled, and repurposed, ensuring that all components are handled according to sustainability guidelines.

By maintaining a record of each product's lifecycle on the blockchain, companies can also verify compliance with environmental standards, especially for products that are legally required to meet recycling quotas or eco-labeling requirements.

Incentivizing Recycling Through Tokenization

Blockchain-based tokenization can incentivize customers to participate in recycling programs. For example, companies can issue digital tokens to customers who return products for recycling. These tokens could be redeemed for discounts or rewards, encouraging environmentally responsible behavior among customers.

Tokenization also benefits companies by providing an accurate and traceable record of each recycled product. This data can be used to analyze recycling rates, improve sustainability practices, and demonstrate compliance with regulatory requirements for waste reduction.

Example in Action:

Coca-Cola has piloted a blockchain system for tracking plastic recycling in North America. By recording each bottle's lifecycle on the blockchain, Coca-Cola can monitor recycling efforts more accurately and incentivize recycling among consumers through tokenized rewards.

Blockchain technology holds significant potential to improve reverse logistics, enhancing efficiency in returns management, transparency in product refunds, and environmental sustainability in recycling and waste management. Through the use of immutable ledgers, decentralized records, and smart contracts, blockchain can transform how companies handle returns and contribute to more sustainable business practices.

The real-world applications of blockchain in reverse logistics—from managing returns efficiently to encouraging responsible recycling—demonstrate how blockchain's unique features can address traditional pain points in reverse logistics and support more sustainable supply chains. As companies increasingly adopt blockchain for their reverse logistics operations, they can benefit from streamlined processes, reduced costs, and stronger customer relationships, ultimately building a more resilient and responsible supply chain.

Chapter 17: Challenges and Limitations of Blockchain in Inventory Management

- ➤ *Technical Limitations (Scalability, Speed, Energy Consumption)*
- ➤ *Legal and Regulatory Hurdles*
- ➤ *Organizational Challenges: Skills, Costs, and Culture Change*

Blockchain technology presents transformative potential for inventory management by enhancing transparency, improving security, and streamlining supply chain operations. However, the adoption of blockchain in inventory management comes with its own set of challenges and limitations. These obstacles range from technical issues, such as scalability and energy consumption, to legal and regulatory concerns, as well as organizational challenges related to costs, workforce skills, and cultural changes. This chapter will explore the key challenges that companies face when implementing blockchain in inventory management and discuss potential ways to address or mitigate these issues.

Technical Limitations of Blockchain

Blockchain technology is revolutionary, but it also has several inherent technical limitations that can pose challenges for inventory management applications. Understanding these limitations is essential for organizations seeking to implement blockchain effectively in their inventory systems.

Scalability

Scalability is one of the most significant technical hurdles in blockchain technology, especially for public blockchain networks like Bitcoin and Ethereum. These networks rely on consensus mechanisms, such as proof of work (PoW), to validate transactions. While this provides a high level of security, it also slows down transaction processing times. Inventory management systems, especially those used by large-scale operations or global supply chains, require high transaction throughput to manage the movement and tracking of goods in real-time.

For example, a large retailer processing thousands of transactions per second may find that a public blockchain cannot meet its needs. Private and consortium blockchains, which are more scalable, could offer some solutions. However, these blockchains may sacrifice some of the decentralized benefits that make blockchain attractive in the first place.

Speed and Latency

Blockchain transactions, especially on public networks, can take several minutes or even hours to be confirmed. In inventory management, where real-time updates are often crucial, this latency can be problematic. For instance, a shipment might require immediate status updates as it moves between warehouses and retailers. If there is a significant delay in recording or accessing data on the blockchain, it could lead to inefficiencies and reduce the effectiveness of blockchain in real-time inventory tracking.

Some blockchains, such as Solana and Algorand, have developed faster consensus mechanisms that enable quicker transaction processing. However, the adoption of these newer blockchain solutions comes with its own challenges, as they are still evolving, and their long-term stability remains to be seen.

Energy Consumption

Certain blockchain networks, particularly those using PoW as their consensus mechanism, are known for their high energy consumption. This can be a significant drawback for companies focusing on sustainability in their supply chains. PoW-based blockchains like Bitcoin and Ethereum require enormous computational power to validate transactions, which results in high energy consumption.

Energy-intensive blockchain networks may conflict with a company's sustainability goals, particularly if the company is committed to reducing its carbon footprint. Fortunately, alternative consensus mechanisms, such as proof of stake (PoS) and proof of authority (PoA), are more energy-efficient and could offer a viable solution for companies looking to adopt blockchain for inventory management without compromising their environmental objectives.

Legal and Regulatory Hurdles

The decentralized and borderless nature of blockchain technology presents unique legal and regulatory challenges. As companies implement blockchain for inventory management, they must navigate a complex and evolving regulatory landscape.

Data Privacy and Compliance

One of the key regulatory issues surrounding blockchain is data privacy. Since blockchain transactions are often transparent and immutable, they can pose a challenge for companies that need to comply with data protection regulations such as the General Data Protection Regulation (GDPR) in the European Union. GDPR requires organizations to give individuals the "right to be forgotten," which conflicts with blockchain's inherent immutability.

For example, if a customer requests the deletion of their personal information from an inventory management system on the blockchain, it would be challenging to remove the data without undermining the integrity of the blockchain. Solutions like zero-knowledge proofs and privacy-preserving blockchains are emerging, but they are still in their infancy and may not yet provide comprehensive solutions to privacy concerns.

Jurisdictional and Cross-border Issues

Blockchain operates on a decentralized network that can span multiple countries, making it challenging to determine the jurisdiction governing transactions and data storage. This lack of clear jurisdiction can lead to legal uncertainties, especially in cross-border inventory management and supply chain operations. Different countries have different regulations regarding data handling, cryptocurrency, and smart contracts, which could complicate blockchain's implementation in global inventory systems.

Smart Contract Legality

Smart contracts, a key feature of blockchain, offer a way to automate transactions based on pre-set conditions. However, the legal status of smart contracts is still ambiguous in many jurisdictions. For instance, a smart contract for an inventory transaction could be subject to legal scrutiny, as some countries may not recognize digital contracts as legally binding. This lack of legal clarity can be a barrier for companies considering blockchain for automated transactions in inventory management, as they may face legal challenges if smart contracts are not enforceable.

Organizational Challenges: Skills, Costs, and Culture Change

Apart from technical and regulatory barriers, the successful implementation of blockchain in inventory management requires overcoming several organizational challenges. These include the need for skilled personnel, the high costs associated with implementation, and the cultural shift required to embrace decentralized technology.

Skills and Talent Gap

Implementing blockchain technology requires a skilled workforce with expertise in blockchain development, data analytics, and cybersecurity.

However, there is currently a shortage of professionals with specialized knowledge in blockchain. Most organizations lack in-house blockchain expertise, and hiring external consultants or training existing employees can be costly and time-consuming.

In addition to blockchain-specific skills, employees also need to understand how blockchain integrates with inventory management systems and supply chain operations. Training programs, partnerships with technology firms, and collaboration with academic institutions can help address this talent gap, but the process may be lengthy and resource-intensive.

Implementation Costs

The costs associated with implementing blockchain in inventory management can be significant. Setting up a blockchain infrastructure involves expenses related to hardware, software, and network resources. For larger companies, the initial costs of transitioning from a traditional inventory system to a blockchain-based system can be prohibitive. There are also ongoing operational costs, such as transaction fees, network maintenance, and energy consumption (especially for PoW blockchains).

Smaller organizations or companies with limited budgets may struggle to justify these expenses, particularly if the benefits of blockchain are not immediately apparent. Conducting a cost-benefit analysis and exploring cost-effective blockchain options, such as consortium blockchains, may help companies determine whether blockchain is a viable solution for their inventory management needs.

Cultural Resistance to Change

Blockchain represents a fundamental shift from centralized to decentralized systems, which can be challenging for companies accustomed to traditional inventory management practices. The implementation of blockchain often requires a shift in mindset, with employees and stakeholders needing to embrace new ways of working, increased transparency, and decentralized decision-making.

This cultural change can be met with resistance from employees who may be wary of adopting new technologies or from management who may be reluctant to relinquish centralized control. To successfully implement blockchain, companies must invest in change management strategies, provide clear communication about the benefits of blockchain, and foster a culture that values innovation and adaptability.

While blockchain offers exciting possibilities for inventory management, its adoption is not without challenges. Technical limitations like scalability, speed, and energy consumption, along with legal and regulatory complexities, can hinder the effectiveness of blockchain solutions in inventory systems. Additionally, the skills and cost requirements, combined with the need for cultural adaptation, present organizational challenges that companies must overcome.

Despite these obstacles, companies that proactively address these challenges can still harness the transformative potential of blockchain for inventory management. By selecting the right type of blockchain, investing in training, and fostering an innovative culture, organizations can position themselves to benefit from blockchain's advantages while mitigating its limitations. The key to successful blockchain implementation lies in a balanced approach that carefully considers both the opportunities and challenges that this technology presents.

Chapter 18: Practical Guide to Blockchain Implementation

- *Steps to Begin Blockchain Adoption in Inventory Systems*
- *Choosing Blockchain Service Providers and Technologies*
- *Roadmap for Successful Integration and Long-term Success*

Implementing blockchain technology in inventory management offers the potential for increased transparency, better data security, and operational efficiencies. However, to achieve these benefits, companies must carefully plan and execute a structured approach for blockchain adoption. This chapter provides a practical guide to starting blockchain implementation in inventory systems, choosing the right technology and service providers, and creating a roadmap for successful integration and sustained growth.

Steps to Begin Blockchain Adoption in Inventory Systems

The initial phase of adopting blockchain in inventory management is crucial. It requires an understanding of the technology's potential impact, the specific pain points in the current inventory system, and a strategic approach to integration.

Identify Pain Points and Define Objectives

Before implementing blockchain, it's essential to identify specific challenges within the existing inventory management system. For example, are there issues with data accuracy, transparency, or tracking product authenticity? Define clear objectives for the blockchain project, whether they are improving traceability, reducing costs, or automating inventory transactions. This clarity will help set measurable goals and justify the investment in blockchain.

Conduct Feasibility Studies

Blockchain might not be the right solution for every problem, so conducting feasibility studies is critical. Evaluate the technical requirements, cost implications, and potential limitations. A feasibility study should assess whether blockchain's advantages outweigh its challenges for the particular inventory system in question.

Engage Stakeholders and Build a Cross-functional Team

Blockchain adoption is not just a technical project; it requires buy-in from multiple stakeholders. Form a cross-functional team including IT, supply chain management, legal, finance, and operations. This team should collaborate to ensure the blockchain project aligns with the company's broader objectives, while also addressing each department's specific concerns.

Design a Pilot Program

Starting with a pilot program is often the most effective way to implement blockchain without disrupting the entire inventory management system. Select a specific inventory process or product category for the pilot. Define success criteria, such as improvements in tracking accuracy or reductions in fraud, and set a timeline for evaluation. This phased approach allows the team to test blockchain's effectiveness, refine the approach, and address any issues before a full rollout.

Develop a Data Management Plan

Blockchain involves sharing data across a network, so a data management plan is essential. Determine the type of data that will be stored on the blockchain (e.g., inventory levels, shipment dates, supplier details), who will have access to this data, and how it will be kept secure and compliant with regulations like GDPR or CCPA. Also, consider the use of off-chain storage for data that does not require immutability or transparency, which can help reduce costs and improve scalability.

Train Employees and Build Blockchain Literacy

Blockchain introduces new ways of working, and employees must understand its basics, from how transactions are processed to the importance of data integrity. Training programs should be established to improve blockchain literacy, and ongoing learning initiatives can keep the team updated on the latest developments in blockchain technology.

Establish Governance and Compliance Protocols

Blockchain's decentralized nature requires new governance structures. Develop protocols for who can add, update, or verify information on the blockchain, ensuring all transactions align with internal policies and legal regulations. Compliance with data protection laws is especially important, as inventory data often involves sensitive information about suppliers, clients, and transactions.

Choosing Blockchain Service Providers and Technologies

With numerous blockchain platforms and service providers available, selecting the right ones can be a challenge. The choice depends on factors such as the organization's goals, industry requirements, and budget.

Decide Between Public, Private, or Consortium Blockchain

Blockchain networks are classified as public, private, or consortium:

Public Blockchains like Ethereum offer full transparency and decentralization but may not be suitable for inventory management due to scalability and privacy concerns.

Private Blockchains are more secure and scalable, as they restrict access to verified participants. They are often used by companies for internal operations and data management.

Consortium Blockchains involve multiple organizations sharing access, ideal for industry-wide initiatives or partnerships with suppliers. They balance transparency and control, making them suitable for supply chain networks.

Each type has its trade-offs, so select the one that best fits your organization's operational needs and security requirements.

Evaluate Blockchain Platforms

Popular platforms for blockchain in inventory management include Hyperledger Fabric, Ethereum, Corda, and Quorum. Each platform has unique features: Hyperledger Fabric, for example, is well-suited for business environments and offers private channels for sensitive data, while Ethereum is known for its smart contract capabilities and large developer community.

Assess each platform's compatibility with your organization's inventory needs. Factors to consider include transaction speed, ease of integration with existing systems, and support for smart contracts and tokenization.

Select Service Providers or Blockchain-as-a-Service (BaaS) Solutions

Blockchain-as-a-Service (BaaS) solutions from companies like IBM, Microsoft Azure, and Amazon Web Services simplify blockchain deployment by offering pre-built blockchain infrastructure. These services can be cost-effective for companies lacking in-house blockchain expertise.

BaaS providers typically offer customizable templates and built-in security protocols, which can reduce development time and resources. Compare providers based on the specific features they offer, such as integration options, scalability, customer support, and pricing.

Assess Smart Contract Capabilities

Smart contracts are essential for automating inventory transactions and ensuring compliance. Ensure the chosen blockchain platform supports robust smart contract functionality and has a secure, user-friendly environment for coding and deploying contracts.

Consider Long-term Support and Development

Blockchain is a rapidly evolving field, and long-term support is crucial. Evaluate the commitment of the service provider or platform to ongoing updates, security improvements, and technical support. An active community and regular platform updates can indicate that the blockchain solution will continue to meet your needs over time.

Roadmap for Successful Integration and Long-term Success

For blockchain integration to be successful in the long term, a strategic roadmap is essential. This roadmap should outline the steps, timelines, and resources required for effective blockchain implementation.

Define a Clear Timeline with Milestones

Develop a detailed timeline for the blockchain project, including major milestones such as the completion of the pilot phase, system integration, and company-wide rollout. Setting realistic milestones can help track progress and ensure the project remains on schedule.

Ensure Interoperability with Existing Systems

Integration with existing inventory management systems, such as ERP (Enterprise Resource Planning) or WMS (Warehouse Management System), is crucial for smooth operations. Interoperability allows data to flow seamlessly between blockchain and legacy systems, avoiding data silos and improving overall efficiency.

Focus on Change Management

Implementing blockchain requires significant change management to overcome resistance and ensure alignment across departments. Communication strategies should be developed to educate employees on the benefits of blockchain and to address any concerns. Internal champions or advocates can be appointed to lead change initiatives and promote blockchain's advantages within the organization.

Monitor Performance and Conduct Regular Audits

Regular performance monitoring and audits help ensure that the blockchain system functions as intended. Track metrics such as transaction speed, data accuracy, and cost savings to measure blockchain's effectiveness. Conduct periodic security audits to identify vulnerabilities and ensure compliance with relevant regulations.

Plan for Scaling and Upgrades

As blockchain technology evolves, companies may need to scale their systems or implement upgrades to improve performance and incorporate new features. Establishing a strategy for scalability can prevent potential disruptions and ensure that the blockchain infrastructure remains robust as inventory volumes grow.

Encourage Continuous Learning and Innovation

Blockchain technology is still developing, and ongoing learning will be necessary to stay updated on new features, tools, and industry trends. Foster a culture of innovation by encouraging team members to explore new applications of blockchain, attend industry conferences, and participate in relevant training programs.

Engage in Industry Collaboration

Blockchain's impact is magnified through collaboration across the supply chain. By engaging with industry peers, companies can leverage shared learnings, establish best practices, and even develop consortium blockchains for broader benefits. Industry associations or partnerships can also help shape blockchain standards and promote interoperability across different platforms.

Implementing blockchain in inventory management is a multi-step process that requires careful planning, stakeholder engagement, and a focus on long-term success. By following a structured approach—beginning with identifying pain points and selecting the right technology, and continuing through a roadmap that addresses integration, change management, and scalability—companies can maximize the benefits of blockchain while minimizing potential challenges.

The right blockchain solution can deliver significant improvements in inventory accuracy, security, and operational efficiency. With a clear roadmap and commitment to continuous improvement, blockchain can become a powerful tool for modernizing inventory management and achieving sustainable competitive advantages in today's dynamic business environment.

Chapter 19: Future Trends and Innovations in Blockchain for Inventory

- *Blockchain and AI for Predictive Inventory and Demand Planning*
- *DAOs (Decentralized Autonomous Organizations) in Inventory Management*
- *Future of Blockchain-based Inventory Financing and Tokenized Assets*

Blockchain technology has transformed inventory management, bringing enhancements in transparency, security, and operational efficiency. However, the evolution of blockchain is far from over. Emerging trends and innovations are paving the way for even more advanced applications, particularly when combined with technologies like artificial intelligence (AI), decentralized autonomous organizations (DAOs), and asset tokenization. This chapter explores the future possibilities of blockchain in inventory management, focusing on how these trends are likely to impact predictive planning, financing, and organizational structures.

Blockchain and AI for Predictive Inventory and Demand Planning

The integration of blockchain and AI has tremendous potential to reshape predictive inventory management. While blockchain enhances data security and transparency, AI offers powerful tools for analyzing large datasets and making accurate predictions, enabling organizations to anticipate demand more effectively and avoid stockouts or overstock situations.

Leveraging Real-time Data for Accurate Demand Forecasting

Blockchain creates an unalterable, real-time ledger of inventory movements, sales data, and supply chain activities. This wealth of data, when combined with AI algorithms, can provide highly accurate demand forecasts. AI can analyze historical trends, market changes, and real-time sales data to predict future demand, helping inventory managers make more informed decisions. With blockchain providing a single source of truth, these predictions are based on verified data, increasing their reliability.

Automated Inventory Replenishment Based on AI Predictions

Predictive models powered by AI can identify the ideal times to reorder inventory, optimizing stock levels to minimize costs and prevent shortages. Smart contracts on the blockchain can automate the reordering process by triggering purchase orders based on predefined thresholds. This combination of AI-driven insights and blockchain automation ensures inventory remains at optimal levels, with minimal manual intervention, leading to cost savings and reduced operational complexity.

Enhanced Supplier Collaboration with Predictive Insights

Blockchain's transparent nature allows suppliers and retailers to access the same inventory data, fostering collaboration across the supply chain. When combined with AI-based predictive insights, suppliers can adjust their production schedules or shipments to match anticipated demand. This collaboration reduces lead times and helps companies maintain a lean inventory, improving efficiency while reducing the risk of bottlenecks.

Potential of AI for Anomaly Detection

AI can identify unusual patterns in inventory usage, which might indicate issues such as theft, fraud, or demand spikes due to unforeseen events. Blockchain ensures data authenticity, making AI-based anomaly detection even more accurate. Real-time alerts can help inventory managers respond quickly to potential disruptions, thereby safeguarding against unexpected losses and enhancing overall risk management.

DAOs (Decentralized Autonomous Organizations) in Inventory Management

Decentralized Autonomous Organizations (DAOs) operate on blockchain technology, allowing stakeholders to manage and make decisions collectively through smart contracts, without central authority. DAOs have started to gain traction as a governance model and hold exciting possibilities for inventory management by enabling decentralized decision-making and increased collaboration.

Collaborative Decision-Making for Supply Chain Partners

In a traditional setup, inventory management decisions are often centralized within an organization. However, a DAO can democratize decision-making by allowing all supply chain participants to vote on important decisions, such as stock levels, reordering schedules, or quality control measures. This decentralized model promotes transparency and encourages shared responsibility, potentially leading to better inventory outcomes.

Incentivizing Participation and Compliance

DAOs can create token-based incentive systems that reward supply chain participants for timely deliveries, high-quality products, or efficient processes. Tokens may represent rewards, voting rights, or stakes within the organization, incentivizing suppliers and other stakeholders to uphold high standards. This transparent incentive structure enhances accountability, which can lead to better overall supply chain performance.

Flexible and Automated Governance Through Smart Contracts

Smart contracts govern DAOs, automating processes like inventory replenishment, order confirmations, and payment distribution. When specific conditions are met, smart contracts execute actions without manual intervention. For instance, if stock levels fall below a certain threshold, a smart contract can automatically approve a reorder request, benefiting inventory managers by reducing the need for constant monitoring.

Reduced Operational Costs and Improved Efficiency

DAOs minimize the need for intermediaries, reducing administrative overhead and costs associated with traditional inventory governance. Decisions are made collectively, with protocols in place for automatic action, thus allowing more efficient management of resources. This model can be particularly advantageous for companies with complex or multinational supply chains, where traditional hierarchies can slow down decision-making.

Future of Blockchain-based Inventory Financing and Tokenized Assets

Blockchain technology opens up innovative avenues for inventory financing and asset management through tokenization, allowing companies to maximize the utility of their inventory assets while accessing flexible financing solutions. Tokenized assets and blockchain-based financing models can enable quicker access to capital, more efficient asset management, and enhanced liquidity within the supply chain.

Tokenizing Inventory for Enhanced Liquidity

Tokenization involves representing physical assets, such as inventory, as digital tokens on a blockchain. Each token represents ownership or a stake in a specific inventory unit, which can be transferred or traded seamlessly. By tokenizing inventory, businesses can make their stock liquid, enabling them to trade or sell tokens representing inventory to raise funds or settle debts. This liquidity can improve cash flow, especially for businesses with large volumes of slow-moving inventory.

Inventory-backed Financing Through Blockchain

Blockchain-based financing solutions, also known as decentralized finance (DeFi), provide access to funding based on tokenized inventory assets. Businesses can use their inventory tokens as collateral for loans or credit lines from decentralized platforms, bypassing traditional financial institutions. This access to funding can help businesses meet operational needs without selling inventory, especially in industries with high capital requirements.

Supply Chain Token Ecosystems

In the future, entire supply chains may operate as token ecosystems, where each participant has access to a shared pool of tokenized assets. Such ecosystems could allow for seamless asset transfers between suppliers, distributors, and retailers, where each party uses tokens as a unit of exchange. This model not only increases liquidity but also simplifies accounting and reduces the need for complex invoicing processes.

Blockchain-based Inventory Insurance and Risk Management

Blockchain can improve inventory insurance models by providing immutable records of product conditions, storage environments, and handling practices. Tokenized inventory can serve as collateral for insurance policies, with premiums and claims adjusted automatically based on data stored on the blockchain. Such real-time, data-driven insurance models could minimize fraud, ensure faster claims processing, and reduce risk exposure for businesses.

Enhanced Transparency for Investors and Stakeholders

Tokenized inventory on blockchain provides enhanced transparency to investors and stakeholders. Each token corresponds to a tangible asset and is traceable, enabling stakeholders to track the value and condition of inventory assets. This transparency builds trust and can attract new investment, as stakeholders have real-time visibility into the company's inventory value and management practices.

The Path Forward: Navigating the Future of Blockchain in Inventory Management

As blockchain technology matures, its integration with AI, tokenization, and decentralized governance models promises to revolutionize inventory management. Predictive planning, collaborative governance through DAOs, and asset liquidity through tokenization are just a few examples of what the future holds. To fully leverage these innovations, companies should focus on developing agile, forward-thinking strategies that embrace these advancements.

Embrace Continuous Learning and Experimentation

Blockchain and AI are rapidly evolving fields, so companies need to stay updated on the latest advancements. By fostering a culture of innovation and continuously exploring new technologies, companies can stay ahead of the curve and remain competitive.

Invest in Partnerships and Collaboration

The decentralized and collaborative nature of blockchain enables new forms of partnerships across the supply chain. By actively engaging in industry alliances or consortium blockchains, companies can benefit from shared resources, collective problem-solving, and access to blockchain-enabled supply chain networks.

Focus on Data Interoperability and Standards

The success of blockchain and AI integration depends on data interoperability and the establishment of industry standards. Companies should work towards creating systems that can communicate seamlessly across blockchain platforms, ensuring that data can be exchanged, verified, and analyzed efficiently.

Implement Scalable and Flexible Blockchain Infrastructure

As these technologies continue to advance, scalability will remain a crucial consideration. Companies should adopt blockchain solutions that are flexible and capable of supporting growth, whether that means increasing data storage capacities or accommodating more participants within the network.

Prepare for Regulatory Changes

Innovations like DAOs and tokenization are still relatively new, and regulatory landscapes are evolving to accommodate them. Companies should monitor regulatory developments closely, ensuring compliance while adapting to any new laws that govern blockchain, digital assets, and decentralized governance.

The future of blockchain in inventory management holds exciting possibilities. By combining blockchain with AI, companies can create predictive, transparent, and automated inventory systems that improve efficiency and reduce operational risks. DAOs offer a new governance model for managing inventory collaboratively, while tokenization and decentralized financing present opportunities to increase asset liquidity and provide flexible financing solutions.

As companies continue to explore these innovative applications, blockchain's role in inventory management will grow, driving new standards for efficiency, transparency, and resilience in the supply chain. By staying adaptable, embracing technological advancements, and preparing for an increasingly decentralized future, organizations can position themselves to thrive in this rapidly evolving landscape.

Chapter 20: Preparing for a Blockchain-enabled Inventory Future

- *Embracing a Blockchain-driven Culture of Transparency and Accountability*
- *Strategic Foresight: Preparing for Technology Advancements*
- *Final Thoughts on Blockchain's Role in the Future of Inventory Management*

The rapid adoption of blockchain technology is transforming inventory management, offering unparalleled transparency, accountability, and efficiency. As we look to the future, preparing for a blockchain-enabled inventory system requires more than just technological upgrades; it demands a shift in organizational culture, strategic foresight, and a comprehensive understanding of blockchain's long-term implications. This final chapter explores how organizations can embrace a culture of transparency, prepare for technological advancements, and the future of blockchain in inventory management.

Embracing a Blockchain-driven Culture of Transparency and Accountability

The successful implementation of blockchain in inventory management goes beyond technical adoption. It requires a shift in organizational culture toward greater transparency, accountability, and trust.

Building a Culture of Transparency

Blockchain's decentralized ledger technology offers unparalleled transparency by providing an immutable record of each transaction. This visibility enables every stakeholder in the inventory process—suppliers, warehouse managers, retailers, and customers—to access real-time, verified data. For many companies, this level of openness is a departure from traditional practices. To fully leverage blockchain, companies must foster a culture that values and supports transparency.

Embracing transparency means allowing visibility into every aspect of the inventory lifecycle. Employees should be encouraged to view transparency as a tool for improvement rather than as a means of surveillance. When inventory data is accessible to all stakeholders, potential issues—such as delays, shortages, or discrepancies—are easier to identify and address collaboratively, reducing the risk of errors and inefficiencies.

Accountability at Every Level

With blockchain, each action is permanently recorded and visible to all authorized parties, making accountability an inherent part of the system. The certainty that each participant's actions are traceable fosters greater responsibility, as employees and partners know that their contributions are visible and verifiable. Establishing a culture of accountability involves clearly defining roles and responsibilities in inventory management and ensuring each team member understands how their actions impact the broader supply chain.

Encouraging Ethical Practices

Blockchain can enforce ethical practices by making it difficult to conceal discrepancies, fraudulent activities, or unauthorized changes. As part of a blockchain-driven culture, organizations should encourage ethical decision-making and adherence to industry standards. With a transparent, blockchain-based system, stakeholders have confidence in the integrity of inventory data, strengthening supplier relationships, customer trust, and regulatory compliance.

Supporting Change Management for Blockchain Adoption

A blockchain-driven culture requires ongoing change management, as implementing a blockchain inventory system will affect workflows, roles, and expectations. Providing training sessions, workshops, and resources to help employees adapt to new processes is essential. Moreover, an inclusive approach to change—where employees at all levels are encouraged to provide feedback and suggestions—can help ease the transition and create a more resilient organization.

Strategic Foresight: Preparing for Technology Advancements

As blockchain technology evolves, organizations need to adopt a forward-looking approach to remain competitive and maximize the benefits of blockchain-enabled inventory systems.

Staying Updated on Technological Advancements

Blockchain technology is constantly evolving, with advancements such as Layer 2 solutions, sidechains, and cross-chain interoperability. Staying updated on these developments allows companies to anticipate new applications, understand emerging risks, and take advantage of enhanced capabilities. Inventory managers, IT specialists, and decision-makers should regularly assess the latest blockchain trends and consider how these innovations could impact their systems and processes.

Investing in Skills and Knowledge Development

As blockchain technology reshapes inventory management, the need for specialized skills will grow. Companies should invest in upskilling programs for their workforce, ensuring team members have the knowledge to work with blockchain and understand its implications. For example, employees responsible for inventory management should be familiar with smart contracts, distributed ledger concepts, and security protocols. Developing internal blockchain expertise will enhance the organization's ability to adapt to future technological shifts.

Fostering Cross-functional Collaboration

A successful blockchain implementation in inventory management requires collaboration across various departments, including IT, operations, legal, and procurement. Blockchain's potential to streamline processes and improve transparency impacts many areas, necessitating a cross-functional approach. Establishing a collaborative framework will allow departments to share insights, address common challenges, and create unified strategies for managing blockchain-based inventory systems.

Preparing for Future Integrations with Emerging Technologies

Blockchain has significant synergies with other technologies, such as artificial intelligence (AI), the Internet of Things (IoT), and machine learning. Preparing for a blockchain-enabled future includes strategizing for these integrations to create an interconnected inventory system that can automatically analyze data, make predictions, and trigger smart contract actions. For example, IoT sensors embedded in inventory items can track their condition and location, feeding real-time data into a blockchain, where AI algorithms could use this data to optimize stock levels and replenishment cycles.

Anticipating Regulatory and Compliance Changes

Blockchain's potential for reshaping inventory management also raises new regulatory and compliance considerations. Governments and regulatory bodies worldwide are gradually formulating guidelines on blockchain usage, data privacy, and digital transactions. Companies should monitor these changes and ensure their systems comply with new requirements, especially in industries like pharmaceuticals, food, and finance, where regulatory oversight is particularly stringent.

Developing Scalable Blockchain Infrastructure

As blockchain applications expand, the ability to scale will be essential. Preparing for a future where blockchain underpins inventory management means selecting platforms and systems that can handle increased data volumes, more users, and more complex transactions. Organizations should consider scalability in their initial implementation plans, ensuring that their chosen technology can grow with their business needs.

Final Thoughts on Blockchain's Role in the Future of Inventory Management

Blockchain technology offers a transformative approach to inventory management, with the potential to address many of the traditional challenges in the industry, including lack of transparency, inefficiency, and security vulnerabilities. By embracing blockchain's transparency, accountability, and automation capabilities, companies can build inventory systems that are more resilient, efficient, and adaptable to changing market demands.

As we move towards a blockchain-enabled future, organizations must focus on developing a blockchain-friendly culture, staying agile, and preparing for ongoing technological advancements. This shift involves more than just adopting new tools—it requires strategic foresight, a commitment to ethical practices, and the active support of employees at all levels.

Blockchain as a Pillar of Inventory Resilience and Efficiency

Blockchain's decentralized and immutable nature positions it as a powerful tool for enhancing resilience in inventory management. By providing a shared ledger accessible to all authorized stakeholders, blockchain creates an environment where every action is recorded, verifiable, and auditable. This transparency strengthens trust among supply chain partners, enables more accurate demand forecasting, and ensures compliance with quality standards. For inventory managers, blockchain's role in enhancing resilience and operational efficiency makes it a valuable addition to long-term inventory strategies.

Unlocking New Opportunities Through Technology Convergence

Blockchain's synergy with technologies like AI, IoT, and machine learning opens new doors for inventory innovation. Predictive analytics powered by AI, combined with blockchain's secure and transparent data framework, offers unprecedented visibility into future demand, enabling companies to maintain optimal stock levels and minimize costs. The convergence of these technologies can also enhance product traceability, optimize resource allocation, and enable automated compliance verification, making inventory management more agile and responsive to change.

Fostering Industry-wide Collaboration

Blockchain's role in inventory management is not confined to individual companies; its potential benefits extend across entire industries. With blockchain-enabled supply chains, companies can achieve higher levels of collaboration and trust, sharing accurate data with partners to optimize joint processes and reduce inefficiencies. This collaboration can lead to stronger supplier relationships, streamlined logistics, and a more resilient supply chain ecosystem that benefits all participants.

Positioning for a Blockchain-enabled Future

Preparing for a blockchain-enabled future involves more than upgrading technology. Organizations should cultivate a culture that values transparency, invest in continuous learning, and develop flexible strategies that accommodate technological shifts. By positioning themselves at the forefront of blockchain innovation, companies can build resilient, efficient, and future-ready inventory systems.

In conclusion, the future of inventory management is one where blockchain plays an integral role in driving transparency, efficiency, and accountability. Organizations that embrace blockchain and prepare strategically for its evolution will not only optimize their inventory management processes but also position themselves as leaders in a rapidly transforming industry. By focusing on the cultural, technical, and strategic aspects of blockchain adoption, companies can confidently step into a future where blockchain-powered inventory systems are the standard for excellence and reliability.

"In the rapidly evolving landscape of inventory management, embracing blockchain technology is essential for success. This journey is not just about adopting new tools but fostering a culture of innovation, transparency, and accountability. Each challenge presents an opportunity to learn and grow. By prioritizing collaboration and continuous improvement, you can transform obstacles into stepping stones. Your commitment to leveraging blockchain will not only optimize your operations but also inspire change across the industry. Step boldly into the future—your extraordinary journey begins now!"

www.ingramcontent.com/pod-product-compliance
Lightning Source LLC
Chambersburg PA
CBHW052358220526
45465CB00003BB/1150